CHARLES +

M000289872

EAST TENNESSEE

············· *in* ·············

WORLD WAR II

Dewaine A. Speaks & Ray Clift

*Best wishes to Nancy
and Charles,*

Dewaine Speaks

Ray Clift

THE
History
PRESS

Published by The History Press
Charleston, SC
www.historypress.net

Cover images courtesy of Aluminum Company of America, Tennessee Valley Authority,
Dow Chemical Company and Jack Rouse.

First published 2016

Manufactured in the United States

ISBN 978.1.46711.936.8

Library of Congress Control Number: 2015960000

Notice: The information in this book is true and complete to the best of our knowledge. It is
offered without guarantee on the part of the authors or The History Press. The authors and
The History Press disclaim all liability in connection with the use of this book.

This story is dedicated to the men and women who, in support of the nation's war effort, worked extra-long shifts in the nation's factories between 1941 and 1945. For the first time, the stories of several neighboring East Tennessee industries are combined in this synergistic history.

Often working sixteen-hour days, the largely inexperienced women and oftentimes older men rolled up their sleeves and went about the task of helping defeat the enemy. These workers were asked to produce vast amounts of materiel for the soldiers, sailors and airmen who were fighting in faraway and often strange-sounding places. Without the resolve and tenacity of these workers, victory could not have been realized.

The story is further dedicated to the approximately 2,250 men and women from East Tennessee who never returned from the war and to the 11,000 who received serious wounds. This special dedication also includes those mothers and fathers and sisters and brothers who were never able to visit the final resting places of their fallen loved ones—the family members who were left to speak in somber tones when mentioning those faraway places that most of them would never have the opportunity to see.

To all of those mentioned here, and to the thousands who fortunately returned home, it is the hope of the writers, who were small children when the war ended, that you and your sacrifices—many of which were unbearably hard—will always be remembered.

Contents

CONTENTS

FOREWORD

East Tennessee is generally quiet, peaceful and serene. This is the case whether you are in the mountains, on the lakes or in one of the small towns nestled in the valleys between the ridges. Many of these towns and cities are located along the primary streams feeding the mighty Tennessee River, which flows generally south and west. Yet that seemingly subdued atmosphere is deceiving. East Tennessee abounds with industry, innovation and amazingly productive companies large and small.

In *East Tennessee in World War II*, the authors take a close look at the history of the region during World War II. The many initiatives central to the war effort located in East Tennessee are primary focus areas and demonstrate a strength of purpose that existed here in these otherwise peaceful valleys and ridges.

That Germany sent spies ashore in the United States, both in Florida and New York, and that the designated targets were located in East Tennessee shows that our enemy knew of this pocket of industrial strength. These attempted attacks are little-known situations of the early years of World War II that reached here into America's heartland. Had they succeeded, history would surely be differently written.

That the Japanese also were aware of East Tennessee is indicated by American-educated Japanese general Isoroku Yamamoto, who predicted at the beginning of the war that Japan would lose the war because of America's enormous industrial resources that were being applied to the war effort. Yamamoto said, "I fear all we have done is awaken a sleeping giant and fill him with a terrible resolve." In this volume, we are shown by the authors that the sleeping giants of East Tennessee had been awakened and they were indeed angry.

This comprehensive history goes into many details about various aspects of East Tennessee during the war that have not been compiled into a single volume before. From the involvement of the Federal Bureau of Investigation (FBI) with the attempted spy efforts to the diverse operations in multiple companies in the region, we have a fresh look at the history of the people who supported World War II right here in our communities and cities. Also featured are many of the companies for which they worked in support of the war effort.

Among the many industries included in the history are Aluminum Company of America, Dow Chemical Company (formerly Rohm and Haas Chemical Company), Fulton Sylphon Company, Tennessee Eastman Company, Camel Manufacturing Company and several others, as well as the regional electrical utility, the Tennessee Valley Authority. Also included are insights into how the famous Norden Bombsight was created.

Of course, my area of most interest is Oak Ridge, and the treatment of the Secret City here recognizes the extraordinary and amazing industrial and scientific experiment that was the Manhattan Project. The authors have included details of the project that demonstrate the local, state, national and even international significance that Oak Ridge had from its very beginning throughout the war and after the war as well.

Many references are included to individuals who made decisions that supported the war in various ways to serve from home or to serve through the military. Winning that awful war and stopping the killing was at the heart of all efforts in East Tennessee, and the whole region pulled together in amazing ways. That story is told here in the most effective and inclusive way I have seen.

People here in East Tennessee gave their all in a regional team effort. They did so in such a way that people in today's culture may find hard to understand. That alone makes it important to document the history of the region in support of World War II and the culture of teamwork and collaboration that existed when the nation's freedom was being threatened. Unfortunately, many, even most, of the people who actually lived during those years being documented here are no longer with us. We have lost much information, and we are losing more and more all the time. Oral histories are vital, and I am proud that we have captured many of the past few years that could not be captured today.

The information documented in this book is similar in my mind. It is vitally important to capture the history of the support for the war effort and capture it now, before it is too late and the history is gone forever. Dewaine Speaks and Ray Clift have completed an admirable effort and produced a comprehensive result. Their book is easy to read, yet it is chock-full of detail and facts, many of which have not been published previously in the comprehensive manner included here and in the context of World War II history.

I am most proud to have been asked to write the foreword for what I believe will become one of the classic histories of East Tennessee during World War II. Little-known facts are presented in concise and precise terms, making this a truly valuable reference work for future research.

So, I highly recommend this work of historical research to you and invite you to enjoy the benefit of the efforts of the authors. It will become one of your best sources of information about East Tennessee's impact on the diverse initiatives supporting the war efforts.

—Ray Smith, Y-12 National Security Complex Historian

PREFACE

The noise, the awful noise, started at 4:45 a.m. on September 1, 1939. Within an hour, nearly everyone in Poland heard the churning sound of the heavy German bombers and the clatter of the strafing fighter planes. Few were surprised because the military buildup of the Nazis had been obvious for some time. Nonetheless, a war that would eventually envelop 100 million people worldwide had begun. The Poles knew that they were a chip, a very weak chip, that happened to be the first of many chips that would fall. Their resistance lasted only a few days. All of Central Europe would fall within the next few months.

The ominous Axis Alliance agreement was signed in 1940 and had the effect of uniting Japan, Germany and Italy. The Japanese were already fighting with the Chinese and expanded this war when they attacked America's naval fleet at Pearl Harbor, Hawaii, early in the morning of December 7, 1941.

Most Americans were listening to their radios, or a neighbor's radio, as their president told them, "Yesterday, December 7, 1941, a date that will live in infamy, the United States of America was suddenly and deliberately attacked by naval and air forces of the Empire of Japan."

In a time of powerful speeches by leaders of the world, Winston Churchill said, "You ask, what is our aim? I can answer in one word: Victory. Victory at all costs. Victory in spite of all terror. Victory however long and hard the road may be. For without victory there is no survival." President Roosevelt added, "No man can tame a tiger by stroking it. There can be no appeasement with ruthlessness. There can be no reasoning with an incendiary bomb. We know now that a nation can have peace with the Nazis only at the price of total surrender."

Four days after the Japanese struck Pearl Harbor, and after the United States had declared war on Japan, Germany declared war on the United States. This meant that America now had three enemies—it faced another world war. Its army and navy were undermanned, and much of its equipment had become obsolete. Millions of volunteers quickly joined the military from each state. Millions of others would be drafted. Their numbers would reach over 16 million, or 10 percent of the 160 million American population. About 350,000 women would join the armed forces. About 400,000 service men and women would lose their lives.

When Americans learned that much of their Pacific fleet rested on the ocean floor, the indescribable sick-to-the-stomach feeling that swept across the country was only somewhat relieved by the burning resolve to somehow fight back. The desire was there, but no one knew exactly how. How could they quickly train thousands of pilots, tank commanders and submarine crewmen? How could they possibly get industry up and running so it could produce the materiel to support the gigantic military buildup that was just starting?

The industrial complex in East Tennessee was a microcosm of the nation. Few locations in the country had as many war-related industries in such a small geographical area. Most of the manufacturing plants in the area, similar to those across the country, were expanded and modernized. For other military needs, such as nuclear fuel for splitting the atom as part of the Manhattan Project, the largest building in the world at the time was hastily constructed in Oak Ridge, Tennessee.

This work combines the stories of East Tennesseans who fought, as well as those who worked to provide everything needed for the fight. It also tells of the families left behind, families that endured hardships of their own. Recognizing the importance of these who never made it to the battlefield, a well-known but appropriate quote certainly applied: "They also serve who only stand and wait."

Acknowledgements

S pecial thanks for the valuable cooperation and assistance of the following entities:

Aluminum Company of America
Eastman Chemical Company
Holston Army Ammunition Plant
Federal Bureau of Investigation
Fulton Bellows Company
Dow Chemical Company (formerly Rohm and Haas Chemical Company)
Y-12 National Security Complex
Tennessee Valley Authority
United States Air Force
Library of Congress
National Archives
McClung Historical Collection
Knox County Public Library
City of Oak Ridge Public Library
City of Chattanooga Public Library

The following individuals also deserve thanks for their important assistance:

Jack Webb
Gordon Thomas

ACKNOWLEDGEMENTS

Jack Westbrook
David Speaks
Ellen Baldwin Speaks
Dan Harrison
Charlie Murphy
Howard Samples
Ruth Fulton Tiedemann
Worth Campbell
Rebecca Bottoms
Jack Rouse
Jerry Browning
Jim Reed
Rex Davis
Carol Bishop Clift
David Lazar
Ray Smith
Pat Ezell
Kathy Cole
Angela Bell
Robert Bottoms
Jerry Riggs
Marcella Finch
Jim Hackworth
Sanya Tingle
Clara Arban Murphy
Richard Long
Brian McWilliams

INTRODUCTION

In 1942, eight German saboteurs rode in the cramped quarters of two different submarines before finally reaching their American destinations. Four were put ashore on Long Island in New York, while the other team of four was placed on the beach just south of Jacksonville, Florida. Their targets included several vital defense industries, some of which were located in the valley of the Tennessee River.

The number-one target on their list was the Aluminum Company of America's largest plant, which was located in Alcoa, fifteen miles south of Knoxville, Tennessee. When the twentieth century had begun, the Germans were the only producer of what is now called aluminum. By the 1930s, however, the Aluminum Company of America had developed the process and was making the vital aluminum needed for the wings and fuselages for all of America's fighter, bomber, cargo and transport airplanes.

Additionally, the Tennessee Valley Authority dams were of interest to the saboteurs, seven of which were hastily built between 1940 and 1945. It was well known by the leaders in Germany and Japan that these dams were of importance because of the ravenous appetite for electricity of the several defense-related industries in the Tennessee Valley, and others being rapidly built. For instance, by the time the atomic bomb was developed, the government complex in Oak Ridge, Tennessee, alone was consuming more than 20 percent of the total power generated by TVA dams—more than either Los Angeles or New York required.

In the 1930s, forward-thinking management at Philadelphia's Rohm and Haas Chemical Company (now Dow Chemical Company) predicted correctly that war was approaching, and they could clearly see the military advantages that their just-developed product offered when compared to regular glass. Used for canopies on fighter planes, gun blisters on bombers and as lenses for periscopes on submarines, Plexiglas offered the advantage of being shatter-proof, meaning fewer shards of glass would be flying around the aircraft crew when their windshields or gun ports were penetrated. It also provided a clear, undistorted sight of targets because, as opposed to real glass, it would not cause light to curve when passing through.

To help with the production demands from the air corps and navy, the company built a manufacturing plant in Knoxville, Tennessee. With this added capacity, the company was ready to produce the vast quantities of Plexiglas that the military would desperately require. Ultimately, airplane windshields, canopies and turrets for gun ports would be needed for 98,000 fighter planes, 96,000 bombers and thousands of cargo and transport planes. The total number of airplanes built for the various military services during World War II would reach approximately 300,000.

Tennessee Eastman Chemical Company (now Eastman Chemical Company) in Kingsport, Tennessee, had quickly developed an explosive that had 50 percent more power than TNT. It was called RDX for Research Development Explosive. When mixed with TNT, it was called Composition B. This composition was used extensively in bombs and projectiles. RDX was the world's most powerful explosive prior to nuclear weaponry. It was produced in the easily transportable shape of candy kisses.

The Fulton Sylphon Company, located in Knoxville, Tennessee, had furnished metal bellows that enabled the navy's depth charges used during World War I to explode at a precise depth. Because of its relationship with the company, the War Department had stayed in touch with the company in case another war came. The Second World War did become a reality, and the ensuing wartime production by men considered too old to fight and the largely inexperienced women startled the navy liaison officers stationed at their factory. The Swiss scientist Carl Norden used Weston Fulton's invention, the seamless metal bellows, as the heart of his famous bombsight. Norden's company manufactured ninety thousand bombsights and sold them to the government for $8,800 each. The bombsight was America's second-most important secret of the war, yet despite heavy security, its plans were stolen by German spies and smuggled aboard steamships bound for the Fatherland.

Camel Manufacturing Company, located in Knoxville, produced tens of thousands of tents and many other items for the army. Some of these items included parachute harnesses, canteen holders, cartridge belts, backpacks and tops for trucks and Jeeps.

Other area companies played similar but smaller roles. Patent Button Company manufactured millions of buttons for military uniforms and thousands of medals for each branch of service. Appalachian Mills Company turned out wool uniforms and heavy coats for the army. W.J. Savage supported the Fulton Company by furnishing machined parts that were part of some of the bellows assemblies that the Fulton Company was producing. Bell Engineering Company made instruments for aircraft and supplied precision components for Norden's bombsight.

With an unprecedented requirement for electricity, an ample water supply for cooling purposes and a need for strict secrecy, the government chose remotely located Oak Ridge, Tennessee, just twenty miles from Knoxville to produce the nuclear fuel for the first atomic bomb—the nation's number-one secret of the war. The atomic bomb would eventually end the war, but first eighty thousand workers would be required to build the facilities that would enable it to happen. Later, thousands of production workers, many of them inexperienced young women freshly graduated from high schools around the nation, were hired to operate equipment at the plants.

Of the tens of thousands of people who worked on the project, only a few hundred knew the real reason for the massive complex they were building. These were mostly the physicists who had taken part in the splitting of the atom and other scientists who were thought to be able to keep a secret. The remaining thousands of workers were told nothing except to never speak of their job or ask any questions. The few who did ask questions or appeared to be overly curious were promptly sent home.

The first atomic bomb containing nuclear fuel that was enriched in Oak Ridge detonated at 1,890 feet altitude. When secrecy was removed, it was learned that bellows invented by the valley's Weston Fulton were part of the systems on both bombs that initiated the explosion at the desired altitude.

Tennessee National Guard's 117th Infantry Regiment, part of the Army's 30th Division, had been activated in 1940 and was fully trained and at full strength when the war started. More than 300,000 Tennesseans would serve in the armed services. A total of 5,731 would give their lives. About 2,500 were from East Tennessee, and 6 would receive the Congressional Medal of Honor. One of those, Troy A. McGill, would have a highway named in his honor.

CHAPTER 1

TENNESSEANS
PRIOR TO THE WAR

The establishment by Congress of the Tennessee Valley Authority (TVA) in May 1933 would change the face of East Tennessee more than any event since the settlers' arrival a few hundred years before. Norris Dam was the first of a series of dams that would be constructed in an effort to control flooding downstream and provide abundant and economical power.

In the 1930s, like several other southern states, Tennessee surprisingly still suffered from rampant malaria. The number of malaria cases began a steady decline with better flood control and insecticide treatment by TVA. By 1935, all of the agency's employees were required to have vaccinations against malaria and typhoid. By 1947, malaria in the entire state had been completely eliminated.

On Sunday afternoon drives, families would come from miles around to see the massive dam, which was named in honor of George Norris, a Nebraska senator who had championed the TVA cause. Completed in 1936, the dam's large gates were closed by telephone order by President Franklin Roosevelt from the White House.

The economy was quickly helped when fishermen started buying boats, rods, reels and minnows as they enjoyed the lake, which had a shoreline of more than five hundred miles. Also in 1933, Congress established the Great Smoky Mountains National Park. The park was officially opened with a speech delivered by Roosevelt from the top of the mountains. Honeymooners from several states started choosing the sleepy little mountain resort town of Gatlinburg as their first destination together.

Further, in 1933, Congress passed the first of President Roosevelt's "New Deal" programs. The Civilian Conservation Corps (CCC) sought to employ young men and give them a chance to learn new skills. Another unstated goal was to reduce the amount of crime by reducing the number of unemployed people.

Those who joined the program were called "enrollees" and would eventually number about 3 million. More than seventy thousand of these were Tennesseans. The men, seventeen to twenty-eight years of age, had to be single, in reasonably good health and unemployed for at least two months. They were paid thirty dollars a month, and twenty-five dollars of this went home to their parents or into a War Department savings account to be held until the individual received his "honorable discharge."

The work that the CCC did included such things as reforestation, road construction, soil conservation and flood control. Much like the regular military, the enrollees were provided with the basics of food, clothing, shelter and healthcare. Some received vocational training and additional education.

The program lasted for ten years and especially benefited those in areas of chronic structural unemployment. The program was never officially canceled, but after 1942, when the government started dealing with the heavy financial needs of the war effort, the CCC received no funds and was allowed to wither away.

Every community, including some that were very small, had a baseball team. Many of those players in East Tennessee had no uniform, except possibly a common cap—red was a favorite color.

So, this was East Tennessee as the 1930s turned into the 1940s—proud but poor. For most families, their social lives revolved around church, Sunday school and an annual fundraising pie supper at the local school. Their deep faith had helped them through the terrible Depression that had held a particularly firm grip on the area for a decade. The Depression was showing some signs of easing, and hope for the future was strong.

Hope for Tennesseans suddenly turned into anxiety on that Sunday when they learned of the catastrophe at Pearl Harbor. For the next several days, concerned people in large numbers would visit those neighbors who were fortunate enough to own radios and could listen to the news casts. Like Americans everywhere, East Tennesseans yearned to do something important to help return the fight to the country's new enemies. History will show that they succeeded.

Interestingly, and by sheer coincidence, one of the first Americans to become alarmed by the threat posed by Germany was Tennessee's governor,

Young East Tennesseans in a CCC camp. *Courtesy Tennessee Valley Authority.*

Prentice Cooper. He attended a Rotary-sponsored tour of Europe in 1937 and had a personal meeting with Adolf Hitler. After discussions with Hitler, and after noting the obvious massive German military buildup, he became alarmed and convinced that war was inevitable.

Because of the governor's strong misgivings, in 1940 Tennessee became the first state to establish a state defense organization: the Advisory Committee on Preparedness. Then, in January 1941, the state legislature created what was called the Tennessee State Guard. This organization would provide security for the state during the absence of units of the Tennessee National Guard. One of these National Guard units, the 117th Infantry Regiment, would serve with distinction during the war that was soon to start.

With Governor Cooper's recommendation, Tennessee designated vast tracts of land for future use as military bases. Camp Campbell, now Fort Campbell, would be created on some of this land north of Nashville. In 1941, the state purchased more than three thousand acres of land near Smyrna that would become the site of Seward Air Base.

Left: Canned vegetables from a family garden. *Courtesy Jack Rouse.*

Below: Typical 1930s kitchen appliances. *Courtesy Jack Rouse.*

Young lady making soap. *Courtesy Jack Rouse.*

In June 1941, still six months before the war started for America, Major General George S. Patton conducted armored maneuvers on State of Tennessee–provided land. The massive "Tennessee Maneuvers," headquartered at Cumberland University in Lebanon, was conducted over the land in a total of twenty counties. More than 800,000 men and women took part in these training exercises. More than $4 million worth of property

Rural East Tennesseans. *Courtesy Tennessee Valley Authority.*

East Tennessee home, 1930s. *Courtesy Tennessee Valley Authority.*

damage claims were filed. Officially, it was announced that the training was taking place "somewhere in Tennessee."

Before World War II, the Volunteer State was largely rural and relatively poor, as were most of the southern states. Because of this common economic state, some young men had joined the National Guard to earn a little extra money. The congressionally mandated TVA was still young, and the economic benefits that it would bring had not yet been fully realized.

Large numbers of Jews fleeing Hitler's anti-Semitic laws, humiliation and death camps chose Tennessee as a place to try to begin their new lives. To gain entry into the United States, the refugees had to have a sponsor—someone who was willing to offer them a job. Several Tennessee companies showed their "volunteer" spirit when they readily responded with offers of lifesaving jobs for thousands of desperate people.

In several ways, people in the State of Tennessee were in the war before actual fighting started. Many in East Tennessee at that time, of course, had no way of knowing that they would eventually figure prominently in bringing the war to an abrupt end.

CHAPTER 2

UNDER THE WATCHFUL EYE
OF THE ENEMY

The several defense-related industries in the Tennessee Valley had not gone unnoticed by America's new enemies, who were very much aware of the strategic importance of the area. Because of this, the enemy leaders immediately started plotting ways to gain as much intelligence as possible about the factories and at the same time began formulating plans to cripple or destroy them.

Several members of the Japanese hierarchy had gone to college in the United States and knew the country well. Admiral Yamamoto, Japan's premier naval officer, had attended Harvard University from 1919 to 1921. His major studies were in the oil industry, and because he was an outstanding student, he was offered a job in the United States upon his graduation. From 1926 through 1928, he was back as Japan's naval attaché in Washington, D.C. As such, he traveled extensively as he learned about America's business practices and social customs. Admiral Yamamoto would die later in the war because American intelligence services had broken Japan's secret communications code. By decoding Japanese dispatches, the admiral's location for a certain day and time was discovered, and two P-38 fighter planes were at that location awaiting the arrival of his plane. This action proved to be a mixed blessing. While one of Japan's highest officers was no longer available to it, it was obvious to the Japanese from this action that the Americans had broken their code, and they immediately switched to another, more complex code.

In the late 1930s, the German government furnished one-way steamship tickets to Germany for any of their former citizens living in the United States, willing to repatriate back to the Fatherland. Because economic conditions were still miserable in the United States, and because many thought that Germany's economy appeared to be looking up under Hitler's regime, several thousand people moved back to Germany. So, the leaders of Germany and Japan had access to many knowledgeable people, many of whom had firsthand experience inside American industries and who undoubtedly warned of the industrial potential of their American adversary.

Because of this knowledge, Adolf Hitler was persuaded to send well-trained saboteurs to the United States. He ordered that only those who had previously lived there and spoke perfect English be considered for these missions. On the day that Germany declared war on the United States, December 11, 1941, the Fuehrer authorized the financing and training for Operation Pastorius. This mission would be under the direction and planning of the chief of the German *abwehr* (military intelligence), Admiral Wilhelm Canaris, whose spies had been instrumental in the Nazi conquest of Czechoslovakia, Poland, the Netherlands and France.

By the time the saboteurs were sent to the shores of the United States, Germany had been at war with other European countries for three years, and their own factories were starting to have trouble keeping up with the needs of their *wehrmach*. Somewhat surprisingly, Adolf Hitler, in a speech delivered by radio and directed at average German people, for the first time came close to publicly admitting to possible shortages in military supplies. With this in mind, he went on to point out the importance of Germany's own war-related industries:

> *The people at home know what it means to be in snow and ice at a temperature of 35, 38, 40, and 42 degrees below zero, in order to defend Germany. And, because they know it, they are anxious to do whatever they can. It is my duty to issue the summons: Germans at home! Work, produce arms, produce munitions. More arms, and more munitions! By doing so, you will save the life of many a comrade at the front. Produce, and work at our means of transportation, so that everything will get to the front.*

Eight saboteurs on two different German submarines who carried fake driver's licenses, bogus draft deferment cards, counterfeit Social Security cards and fake birth certificates, along with $175,000 cash (more than $2 million in today's dollars), traveled for seventeen days in cramped submarines.

Saboteur's timer for detonating explosives. *Courtesy Federal Bureau of Investigation.*

During the night of June 12, 1942, *U-202* pulled within fifty feet of the beach near Amagansett, New York. George Dasch, Ernst Burger, Richard Quirin and Heinrich Heinck were rowed ashore on rubber rafts by seasoned sailors from the submarine. A line was attached to the rubber boat so the sailors would be able to find their way back to the submarine in the darkness.

The four were spotted on the beach and confronted by a Coast Guardsman while they were attempting to conceal explosives and other equipment in the sand dunes along the shore. They were able to talk their way past him and managed to catch a Long Island Railroad train to a hotel room in Manhattan that was likely reserved for them by a rapidly growing network of Nazi spies, headquartered on Seventy-second Street in New York City.

The unarmed Coast Guardsman, John Cullen, was threatened with his life if he told of their presence and at the same time had $260 in cash stuffed in his hand as the Germans were quickly fleeing the scene. As soon as he was a safe distance away from the Germans and hidden by dense fog, Cullen rushed quickly to the nearest Coast Guard station about five miles away. Several Coast Guardsmen raced to the spot where the Nazis had been spotted just in time to faintly see the submarine in the fog. They did not realize it at the time, but *U-202* was stuck on the bottom on a sandbar. When the fog lifted a few hours later and with a Coast Guard cutter bearing down on them, the submarine narrowly escaped after slowly being lifted with the help of the rising tide.

The Coast Guard superiors then alerted President Franklin Roosevelt. The president called J. Edgar Hoover, director of the Federal Bureau of Investigation, who in turn immediately ordered the launching of a massive manhunt.

Four nights later, on June 16, the second submarine, *U-584*, sneaked close to the shore south of Jacksonville, Florida, at Ponte Vedra Beach. Edward

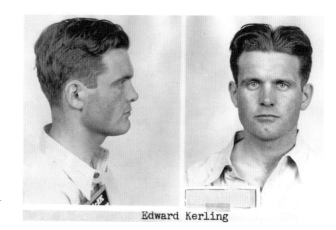

Edward John Kerling.
Courtesy Federal Bureau of Investigation.

Herman Otto Neubauer. *Courtesy Federal Bureau of Investigation.*

Herbert Hans Haupt.
Courtesy Federal Bureau of Investigation.

John Kerling, Hermann Otto Neubauer, Werner Thiel and Herbert Haupt swam ashore wearing bathing suits but quickly changed into civilian clothes. Two boarded a train bound for Cincinnati, Ohio, and two boarded a train headed for Chicago, Illinois. All eight of the saboteurs planned to meet at the Gibson Hotel in Cincinnati on July 4, 1942. After this planned clandestine meeting (which would never take place), the agents had intended to head for military-related industries that were located in New York, Pennsylvania and East Tennessee. Number one on the list of prime targets for the four saboteurs from *U-202* was the Aluminum Company of America plant in Alcoa, Tennessee. This was the largest of the aluminum company's four American installations.

The entire plot started to unravel when Dasch and Burger, realizing it was likely that the FBI had been alerted and was on their trail because of their encounter with Coast Guardsman Cullen, decided to defect to the American government. With Burger remaining in the New York City hotel room that they shared, Dasch took a train to Washington, D.C., to make arrangements for the two to surrender to authorities. He would tell the federal agents that it had been his and Burger's plan to betray the others all along with no intention of ever sabotaging any industries.

Dasch checked into the Mayflower Hotel and went carrying his cash-filled briefcase directly to the headquarters of the FBI, where he asked to see Director Hoover. He was shuffled from agent to agent, with none of them taking him and his seemingly outlandish espionage story seriously. The agents were unanimous in considering the German a crackpot and sought to ignore him and his somewhat unbelievable story.

Finally, Dasch managed to reach the office of the bureau's assistant director, who told him that he was willing to give him just five minutes to tell his story. Dasch, who by then had become quite upset, angrily and abruptly dumped his part of the mission's budget, $84,000 cash, on the top of the assistant director's desk. With this large mound of cash on the desk, the runarounds came to an abrupt halt, and the saboteur was questioned for thirteen hours before being jailed. He would be interrogated for several more days. At this point, Burger, back in New York, was the only one of the espionage agents who was aware of Dasch's betrayal. With Dasch providing the FBI with the locations of the others as well as their friends and acquaintances, Burger and the other six were arrested within two weeks.

J. Edgar Hoover gave a report to President Roosevelt that discussed the arrest of four saboteurs and the pending arrest of the other four that read as follows:

I have taken detailed statements from each of the persons arrested and the story is a startling and shocking one. Long and intensive training is being given by the German authorities to specially selected men who in turn are being placed on board German submarines to be landed on the shores of the United States. The group which landed at Amagansett, Long Island, on June 13, 1942, was the first group to arrive in this country. The second group landed approximately the same time on the coast of Florida. I expect to be able to have in custody all members of the second group. I am definitely informed that additional groups will be sent from Germany to the United States every six weeks to initiate a wave of terror within the United States by the commission of acts of sabotage against many of our key industries, factories, electric power systems and waterworks. I have been able to secure a list of these facilities that were to be included in the first acts of sabotage.

The headline of the *New York Times* announced the capture of all eight Nazis as follows:

FBI Seizes 8 Saboteurs Landed by U-Boats
Here and in Florida to Blow Up War Plants
Invaders Confess
Had TNT to Blast Key Factories

At the time of their capture, the saboteurs were flush with the cash that was supposed to last them for up to two years. During the short time before their capture, they were regularly visiting gambling houses and prostitution establishments. Some looked up old acquaintances. One found an old girl friend and was actually in the process of planning a wedding.

President Roosevelt told his attorney general that he wanted to make examples of the eight in an effort to stop Hitler from any future similar escapades. In a memorandum to Attorney General Biddle, Roosevelt described his thinking at the time:

The two American citizens [Burger and Haupt] *are guilty of high treason. This being wartime, it is my inclination to try them by court martial. I do not see how they can offer any adequate defense. Surely they are guilty as it is possible to be and it seems to me that the death penalty is almost obligatory.*

In the case of the other six who I take it are German citizens, I understand that they came over in submarines wearing seamen's

32

clothes—in all probability German Naval clothes—and that some of them at least landed on our shores in these German Naval clothes. I think it can be proved that they formed a part of the German military or Naval Service. They were apprehended in civilian clothes. This is an absolute parallel of the case of Major Andre in the Revolution and of Nathan Hale. Both of them were hanged. Here again it is my inclination that they be tried by court martial as were Andre and Hale. Without splitting hairs, I can see no difference.

Thinking that a civilian court would likely be too lenient, President Roosevelt issued Executive Proclamation 2561 on July 2, 1942, that created a military tribunal to prosecute the saboteurs. The precedent-setting declaration, in its entirety, reads:

Now, therefore, I, Franklin D. Roosevelt, President of the United States of America and Commander in Chief of the Army and Navy of the United States, by virtue of the authority vested in me by the Constitution and the statutes of the United States, do hereby proclaim that all persons who are subjects, citizens or residents of any nation at war with the United States or who give obedience to or act under the direction of any such nation, and who during time of war enter or attempt to enter the United States or any territory or possession thereof, through coastal or boundary defenses, and are charged with committing or attempting or preparing to commit sabotage, espionage, hostile or warlike acts, or violations of the rules of war, shall be subject to the law of war and to the jurisdiction of military tribunals.

Their trial was held on the fifth floor of the Department of Justice in Washington, D.C., and started on July 8, 1942. Lawyers for the accused attempted to have the case tried in a civilian court but were rebuffed by the Supreme Court in *Ex Parte Quirin*, 317 U.S.1 (1942). This case set the precedent for trial by military tribunal of any unlawful combatant against the United States.

Seven army generals served as the jury in the trial that had no press present and no appeal process available. In spite of everything seemingly going the president's way, Roosevelt reaffirmed to Attorney General Biddle, "I want one thing clearly understood, Francis…[The next time the subject of the saboteurs is brought up,] I won't give them up… I won't hand them over to any United States marshal armed with a writ of *habeas corpus.* Understand?"

Reporters were not allowed to attend the secret proceedings in the courtroom but were allowed inside one day during a recess for about fifteen minutes. They could ask no questions. Still pictures were taken. In order for the reporters to be able to identify each of the defendants, their names were called individually.

One of the reporters in the room, Dillard Stokes of the *Washington Post*, wrote that each of the saboteurs flinched when his name was called aloud. He indicated that Dasch "sat tensely forward on his chair and took notes on a pad on his knee. Kerling gave reporters a long, cold, level stare." Neubauer clasped his hands "so tightly together that his knuckles were white." Haupt "chewed gum vigorously and his mouth curled into a sneer." He noted that "Quirin's wide-set eyes glared." Thiel returned "stare for stare as long as he was under scrutiny." Heinck "did not want to be seen at all and crouched behind a pillar until General Cox ordered him to lean forward."

The trial concluded on August 1, 1942. On August 3, all eight defendants were found guilty and sentenced to death. Based on the recommendation by J. Edgar Hoover, President Roosevelt quickly commuted Dasch's sentence to thirty years and Burger's to life in prison because of their providing information about Operation Pastorius and for turning in the others. The remaining six went to the electric chair on August 8, 1942, and were buried in the Anacostia area of Washington.

Each of the saboteurs was allowed to write a letter two hours before being executed. Eddie Kerling, who was the only one of the condemned to stay verbally committed to Nazism to the very end, wrote the following letter to his wife:

> *Marie, my wife—I am with you to the last minute! This will help me to take it as a German! Even the heaven out there is dark. It's raining. Our graves are far from home, but not forgotten. Marie, until we meet in a better world! May God be with you. My love to you, my heart to my country.*
>
> *Heil Hitler!*
> *Your Ed, always*

Six years later, President Harry S Truman granted executive clemency to Dasch and Burger if they agreed to be relocated to the American zone of occupied Germany. They moved there but were not accepted by the people because they were viewed as traitors who had caused the deaths of their comrades. They both died without ever receiving the pardons that J. Edgar Hoover had long ago promised them.

Operation Pastorius went so poorly that it caused Admiral Canaris to be severely lectured by Hitler and dissuaded the Fuehrer from sending more saboteurs to America until much later in the war. For several months, Admiral Canaris had been strongly opposing the actions of the Fuehrer, and in 1944, he paid for this opposition with his life.

From the time the saboteurs first landed on America's shores, the FBI had been feeding propaganda to the Nazis that made them think that FBI agents had infiltrated the higher echelon of the German intelligence operations. A New York radio station that the Germans thought was under their control was used to feed official-sounding misinformation to the leaders in Germany.

Later in the war, with several reports from his extensive spy network that mentioned "fission," "atoms" and "Manhattan Project," Hitler began worrying about the possibility that the Americans were secretly developing a nuclear bomb. His own scientists, who were also working furiously on making a similar bomb, were telling him that they felt sure that their peers in America were, indeed, closing in on the technology for building such bombs. The Fuehrer was desperate for more information on that project in America. With this in mind, he once again decided to send saboteurs to America's shore. A spy operation that was already being planned that included sending spies to assess the effectiveness of German propaganda was usurped by the new mission. Because of Hitler's growing concern for America's ability to develop an atomic bomb, the main objective now was an attempt to learn as much as possible about what was being called the Manhattan Project.

This time, two saboteurs were sent. Erich Gimpel had been a radio operator in Peru. When Germany declared war on the United States, he became a spy reporting on ship movements around the waters of Peru. For a while, he was a secret agent for the Nazis in Spain. He was then sent to a spy training facility in Hamburg, Germany. While there, he met an American turned spy, William Curtis Colepaugh. Since the raid would take them to the shores of America, Gimpel thought it would be advantageous to team up with Colepaugh, a native-born American spy who was very familiar with his homeland but who spoke almost no German. In turn, Gimpel had a poor command of English. They literally never really understood each other, which perhaps helps to explain why their mission was doomed from the start.

Colepaugh had been in the United States Naval Reserve but defected to the Germans in Lisbon, Portugal. In November 1944, the two German saboteurs, Colepaugh and Gimpel, were dropped off by submarine *U-1230* on the shore near Frenchman's Bay, Maine. Their main objective was to collect information on the status of the Manhattan Project and to sabotage as many munitions factories as possible. As part of their mission called *Unternehmen Elster* (Operation Magpie in English), the two were expected to purchase parts as required and build an eighty-watt radio that they would use to transmit any technical information they were able to obtain back to the Fatherland.

After initially making their way to Boston, Colepaugh and Gimpel traveled by train to New York City. Almost immediately upon reaching American soil, Colepaugh started womanizing and drinking heavily, reminiscent of the other German saboteurs a few years earlier. Then, just like the others, Colepaugh decided to abandon the mission and turned himself in to the FBI. He then revealed everything about their mission and gave information about the expected location of his cohort, who was quickly taken into custody.

As before, the U.S. attorney general formed a military tribunal. Accused of violating the Eighty-second Article of War, the two were found guilty and sentenced to be hanged. They both received a reprieve with the unexpected death of President Roosevelt and the custom of not performing executions during the time of State Mourning. Soon after, the war ended, and their sentences were commuted by President Truman to life terms. By 1944, when Gimpel and Colepaugh came ashore, conditions had changed because Americans were by then themselves sending spies behind enemy lines dressed in civilian clothes, so the death sentence was now less likely for these would-be saboteurs. It was hoped that the Germans would show more mercy on any captured spies if no more of their espionage agents were put to death.

Gimpel, after spending several years in Alcatraz prison, was released in 1955 and returned to West Germany. After the September 11, 2001 attacks on the World Trade Center, Oliver North interviewed Gimpel on North's program *War Stories with Oliver North*. Gimpel died in Sao Paulo, Brazil, in 2010.

Colepaugh was paroled in 1960. He became a model citizen who did work for the Boy Scouts of America and became a member of Rotary. He died in 2005 after battling Alzheimer's disease.

Only after the war ended would the defense workers at many of the targeted defense plants learn that they had been targeted. However, it is unlikely that it would have made any difference to the fiercely determined workers even had they known they were targets and under the watchful eye of the enemy.

CHAPTER 3

ALUMINUM COMPANY OF AMERICA

From the time that man first dreamed of flying, the need for lightweight materials has been of paramount importance. After all, the birds that early aviation pioneers often emulated have hollow bones as part of their design, thus making flight for them much easier to sustain.

Coincidentally, around the turn of the twentieth century, fledgling airplanes and a strong, lightweight material were emerging somewhat simultaneously. The existence of aluminum had been known for centuries. It was given the name aluminum (or aluminium, as it is called in Great Britain) as a derivative from the Latin work *alum*, which means bitter salt. Found in a third century AD tomb in China, a military medal appeared to be made from a strange-looking material. When analyzed, it was determined that it had been made from 85 percent aluminum. There is no record to indicate how this was accomplished at that time by the Chinese.

It was Danish chemist Hans Oersted in Copenhagen in 1825 and German chemist Fredrich Wohler two years later who developed a metal in a form that was pure enough to have its properties fairly evaluated. Oersted's final product was not pure, but a pure final product was produced by Wohlerin in his laboratory when he heated aluminum chloride with potassium.

It was not until 1845 that Wohler was able to produce the material in large enough quantities to establish that it was a very light material that was malleable. This was important, because it meant the material could be shaped or extended by hammering or by pressure applied with rollers. Several decades later, this characteristic would be extremely important.

Ironically, aluminum, this silvery-white, lightweight, malleable and ductile metallic material, is the most abundant element in the earth's crust. It is estimated by geochemists that earth's crust down ten miles consists of 8 percent aluminum. It is found, however, only in combination with other materials. Found mostly mixed in with bauxite, it can also sometimes be found in feldspar, cryolite and clay. The word *bauxite* gets its name from the French town of Les Baux, an area where it was first mined. The ore is found in seven American states, with the largest being located near Little Rock, Arkansas.

Aircraft designers have always faced the need for a favorable weight-to-thrust ratio. Designers of early aircraft quickly saw the property advantages that aluminum provided. They had found that wood and fabric were light but were generally very fragile. They knew that steel was certainly rugged enough but required a disproportionately large power plant. This meant that if the craft got off the ground at all, the rapid fuel consumption by the required large engine would greatly restrict the distance that an aircraft could fly. As fliers often say, "it would have short legs."

Interestingly, when the Wright brothers designed and built their own aircraft engine in 1903, they procured a block of aluminum from the forerunner of the Aluminum Company of America. This engine was machined to have four cylinders and produced twelve horsepower while weighing only 162 pounds.

Aluminum weighs only about one-third as much as most common metals and is very strong. Surprisingly, it has a high melting point of 1,220 degrees Fahrenheit. Only about half as much aluminum is required to yield the same rigidity as steel. A further benefit is that its strength can be greatly increased when alloyed with other metals. Also, although aluminum readily combines with other elements, including oxygen, air does not cause it to rust. Due to a thin film of oxide that forms on the surface, the metal beneath is protected. While it will conduct only about 60 percent of electricity as that of a copper wire of the same size, it will conduct twice as much electricity as a copper wire of the same weight.

An aluminum alloy called Duralim has been relied on heavily since the beginning of flight. Even the zeppelin dirigibles during World War I were largely made of this material. Alfred Wilm, a German engineer, developed the alloy in 1908, which coincided almost perfectly with the early development of aviation. Duralim, perhaps the most important alloy of aluminum, contains about 4 percent copper, 1 percent magnesium and smaller amounts of manganese and silicon. This particular alloy has good strength and lightness but is somewhat susceptible to corrosion. Where corrosion resistance is required, a thin layer of pure aluminum can be applied.

In 1886, French chemist Heroult and Charles Martin Hall, an American, discovered a method of making aluminum on a large scale and fairly inexpensively. Electrolysis of alumina (aluminum oxide) dissolved in a bath of fused cryolite (sodium aluminum fluoride) is the procedure they introduced at about the same time. This method of making aluminum was called the Hall-Heroult Process and was so successful that with a few changes it is still being used.

Prior to entering college, Hall was fascinated by his pastor father's well-worn college chemistry book. At this time, he became extremely interested in a mystery metal: aluminum. A few European chemists had done small experimental work on aluminum. Nothing of practical value came from these experiments. At this time, the material was too scarce and expensive to be used for anything.

While he was still a student at Oberlin College in Ohio, Hall set up an improvised workshop in his family's woodshed. He was able to do some work at school, and one of his teachers, Professor Jewett, became interested in his work and encouraged him to continue. Jewett told his student that fame and fortune awaited the man who could accomplish what the professor thought Hall had likely already been able to do.

Hall spent two years looking for someone to back him and his newly developed product. Finally, an acquaintance introduced him to a small group of businessmen in Pittsburgh with ties to the steel industry. The group, made up entirely of young men, was able to raise $20,000 to invest in Hall's venture. This alliance formed the Pittsburgh Reduction Company.

On Thanksgiving Day 1888, the company poured its first aluminum ingot. Because Hall's manufacturing method allowed the aluminum to be made inexpensively and in large volumes, the price of aluminum started falling rapidly. Previously, it was selling for $17.00 per pound. By 1890, the price had dropped to $2.00. By the turn of the century, it was selling for $0.33 per pound.

Even with all of his technical breakthroughs, Hall found it difficult to sell his product to manufacturers, who were suspicious of the new metal and were averse to change in general. Because of this, the Pittsburgh Reduction Company formed a subsidiary company to produce and sell cookware. Many Americans first became aware of aluminum because of their new aluminum teakettle.

Aluminum ingots. *Courtesy Aluminum Company of America.*

Processing aluminum requires a large amount of electricity. The company built a power plant in Niagara Falls, New York, using the hydroelectricity generated by the falling water. A little later, it built another power plant in upstate New York, with power generated as water cascaded through the rapids of the St. Lawrence River.

Learning that the Pittsburgh Reduction Company was in search of more electric power, the Knoxville Power Company informed it of the vast potential hydroelectric power that was available in East Tennessee. Chairman of the Board Arthur V. Davis came to East Tennessee on a fact-finding mission. He likely came to Knoxville by train and traveled on to Maryville in a horse-drawn wagon.

While on this investigative trip, he observed enough of the Tennessee Valley's hydroelectric potential to fully agree with the assessment of the Knoxville Power Company. On behalf of his company, he immediately began purchasing large tracts of land. In addition to land for a very large production facility, Davis needed land on which to build four hydroelectric dams. By this time, the company had changed its name to the Aluminum Company of America (commonly called Alcoa).

The first Alcoa dam to be completed was at the confluence of the Cheoah River and the Little Tennessee River in 1919. Following in rapid succession was the construction of dams in Santeetlah, Calderwood and Chilhowee. Even with all of this electricity feeding into the aluminum production facility from its privately owned dams, when TVA power became available in the 1930s, the company became a major customer.

Charles Hall did not receive a patent on his innovative aluminum process method until 1909. Even when the term of the patent ended,

Alcoa's Santeetlah Dam. *Courtesy Aluminum Company of America.*

Above: Alcoa plant under construction. *Courtesy Aluminum Company of America.*

Opposite, top: Aluminum rolling mill. *Courtesy Aluminum Company of America.*

Opposite, bottom: Stacks of aluminum ingots. *Courtesy Aluminum Company of America.*

no other company came forward to offer competition. For years, therefore, Alcoa enjoyed a legal monopoly. In 1937, and caught up in the atmosphere surrounding President Roosevelt's New Deal era, there were some who believed that the company should be broken up because of the monopoly.

Litigation was initiated, and the initial decision went in Alcoa's favor. An appellate judge, however, reversed this decision with the pronouncement that Alcoa produced 100 percent of pig aluminum in America, and the only remedy was to encourage the creation of competition. In 1940, with encouragement from the government, Reynolds Metals Company began producing aluminum.

In the 1930s, top management at Alcoa foresaw the likelihood that war was coming and started an aggressive expansion program. A vast production plant was constructed on surrounding farmland. It was called the North

Massive Alcoa equipment. *Courtesy Aluminum Company of America.*

Plant, and when the German saboteurs were captured, one of them had a floor plan of this plant in his possession.

Because the Great Depression still dragged on after more than a decade, most factories were operating at reduced capacity, while others had completely shut their doors. Existing manufacturing plants were encouraged by the government to spring to life to supply the vast amount of war materiel that would be required. The government also started financing the building of new plants to fill the requirements for certain materiel.

Shortly after the war started, Alcoa increased its aluminum production by 200 percent. This increase was not enough to satisfy the large appetite of the military, so the government decided that it would begin making aluminum. Additional plants were built by the government at a cost of $500 million. Alcoa agreed to operate the plants for the government. Its processes, which had taken the company dozens of years to develop, were used in these new plants.

In spite of its patriotic contributions, Alcoa received harsh treatment from the government. At the end of the war, the government decided to

Aluminum processing equipment. *Courtesy Aluminum Company of America.*

Military officers tour the plant. *Courtesy Aluminum Company of America.*

"Miss Aluminum"—tops in war bond sales. *Courtesy Aluminum Company of America.*

sell its aluminum producing plants. Alcoa wanted to bid on the plants but was not allowed to because the government was intent on breaking Alcoa's monopoly. Reynolds Metals Company and Kaiser Company were allowed to buy the plants for thirty cents on the dollar. Alcoa now faced the indignity of having its manufacturing secrets in the hands of its competitors.

Shortly after the war, Senator Stuart Symington of Missouri had the following to say regarding Alcoa's war efforts:

> *The Aluminum Company of America made an outstanding contribution to winning the war, of which this nation should be forever grateful. Your public-spirited action in giving the Government a free license under your alumina patents…is of course less dramatic but nonetheless an equally significant contribution to the winning of the peace.*

The nation quickly became aware of the importance of aluminum during the war years. The Aluminum Company of America's plant started operating at full capacity when President Roosevelt announced his goal in

Sheet aluminum. *Courtesy Aluminum Company of America.*

May 1940 of having 50,000 airplanes built within a year. This was just the start of the 300,000 airplanes that would be built, all requiring aluminum for their wings and fuselages. Because it rose to a very big challenge, *Fortune* magazine would print, "What won the war was air power and Alcoa."

CHAPTER 4

DOW CHEMICAL COMPANY (ROHM AND HAAS CHEMICAL COMPANY)

In the early 1900s, German Otto Rohm submitted his dissertation paper entitled, "The Derivatives of Acrylic Acid." He quickly put his education to work when he started making a product that could be used for tanning hides. It was of great assistance to tanners and soon became popular in that field.

With this promise of success, Dr. Rohm and one of his salesmen, Dr. Fritz Otto Haas, decided to form a business in Stuttgart, Germany, to produce the acid in greater volume. Mr. Haas, who had previously lived in the United States, moved back there in 1917 to produce and sell the popular acid. By 1919, Dr. Rohm had joined him in Pennsylvania, and they founded the Rohm and Haas Chemical Company.

A few years later, Dr. Rohm and Dr. Haas decided to sever their partnership. Rohm returned to Germany and operated a business similar to his former company. Haas's American company introduced a product called Plexiglas at its Bristol, Pennsylvania plant in 1935. At about the same time, Dr. Rohm was also able to make Plexiglas, but unlike the Americans, he and the Germans were never able to produce it in the large volumes that were necessary to have an impact on the war. Consequently, German pilots often went into battle without the benefits that Plexiglas offered.

Plexiglas is not glass at all. It is a special plastic called poly(methyl methacrylate) and has the chemical formula of $(C_5O_2H_8)_n$. It offers the advantages of being lightweight, does not distort light as it passes through and is shatterproof. Plexiglas sheets can be made in different sizes and varying thicknesses and can be clear or colored. It is lighter than aluminum and glass and is practically unbreakable. But it was the shatterproof nature of the product that interested American military leaders, who could see that a war was brewing in the late 1930s. Military applications included aircraft windshields, canopies and blisters for gun turrets. Plexiglas was also used as the lens of periscopes on all American submarines.

Because they were Jewish, several members of Dr. Rohm's family were executed by the Nazis. Rohm himself was harassed by Hitler when the Fuehrer would not believe that Rohm and Haas had really dissolved their partnership. Hitler badly needed American dollars and thought that Rohm could deliver them through his connection with Haas in America. Dr. Rohm was mistreated so badly by the Fuehrer and his regime that some reports say he went insane. Others say he committed suicide.

By the time World War II started, the American military was using vast amounts of Plexiglas. When the Pennsylvania plant could no longer meet the demands of the military, the Defense Plant Corporation of the United States entered into a contract with Rohm and Haas that would establish a government-owned plant for the production of this badly needed plastic.

Grinding and polishing Plexiglas. *Courtesy Dow Chemical Company.*

Left: Polishing Plexiglas at Rohm and Haas plant. *Courtesy Dow Chemical Company.*

Right: Loading a boxcar with Plexiglas sheets. *Courtesy Dow Chemical Company.*

The government selected Knoxville, Tennessee, as the site for the new plant because the site met several strategic criteria. The new plant had to be at least six hundred miles from the coast. The site was required to be near a source of sulfuric acid because so much was used in the process. Fortunately, nearby Copperhill, Tennessee, could produce all that was needed. TVA answered the need for a dependable electricity source. Finally, there was an available building that had previously been used to manufacture construction equipment, and with some modernization efforts, it and the process equipment were ready in eight months to produce the critically needed large amounts of Plexiglas. Indicating the demand for Plexiglas by the military, the new plant's first order was for eighty thousand sheets, which were to be made into airplane canopies.

At the official grand opening of the newest Rohm and Haas plant on July 16, 1943, the corporate secretary and personal confidant of Dr. Haas, Stanton Kelton, made an address to the company employees and members of the press and public. Excerpts from his speech follow:

> *I am proud to bring to you the greetings and good wishes of your 5,000 fellow employees…On July 22, 1942 the authorities in Washington telephoned us to start making Plexiglas in Knoxville as soon as possible. That afternoon orders were placed for more than a million dollars of*

Suggestion box at a Rohm and Haas plant. *Courtesy Dow Chemical Company.*

supplies and equipment. Seven months and nine days later on March 1, 1943—the first sheet of Plexiglas was made in Knoxville.

...special tribute should be rendered to the City Administration of Knoxville, to the Chamber of Commerce, to the Defense Plant Corporation who financed this plant, to the TVA, to the U.S. Employment Service, to the FBI, and to the Army and Navy.

Men and women of Rohm and Haas Company—you have a job to do—no small mean job—and I know you will do it. That job is to make Plexiglas—that job is to make what the Army calls "the eyes of aviation." If each of you could have talked as I have with...men who flew fighter planes at Guadalcanal...men who have had 300 combat hours over Germany and Africa, you would know how much such men treasure the Plexiglas noses and turrets and tail pieces of their planes. You would know that your job will save the lives of thousands of our boys. That job is your job.

We dedicate this new plant of Rohm and Haas with the prayer that it may grow in size and strength, but even more we pray that the men and

Left: Walter Frank Standridge. *Courtesy Dow Chemical Company.*

Right: John Clarence Jarnigan. *Courtesy Dow Chemical Company.*

> *women who make this plant, as generations pass by shall always possess*
> *what a famous historian declared were the outstanding qualities of George*
> *Washington—strength of character and magnanimity. We pray that this*
> *plant may always deserve the respect of this beautiful city of Knoxville.*

That same day, the company was presented an Army/Navy "E" award for excellence banner. During the war, 126 workers from the plant served their country in the military. Two, John Clarence Jarnigan and Walter Frank Standridge, gave their lives.

CHAPTER 5

FULTON SYLPHON COMPANY

Because Weston Fulton and his company had worked with War
Department personnel before and during World War I, when they
worked closely with the navy in developing a depth charge that would
detonate at a desired depth, the government kept the Fulton Company
in mind as being a qualified manufacturer of defense items when and
if another war came. When Germany invaded Poland in 1939, the
government's military readiness panel stepped up its number of visits
to the Fulton Sylphon Company in Knoxville, Tennessee. Engineers,
chemists and other technical personnel were already in place. The facility
had its own foundry, plating shop, fully equipped machine shop, qualified
quality control personnel and a full-time registered nurse. When war
came, it required only the addition of some buildings within the plant
area and the procuring of some heavy press equipment to get production
underway. This sleeping giant was able to awaken quickly because it and
the government committee had done their homework.

Fulton Sylphon Company made hundreds of different items in
support of the war effort, but the one that the military personnel were
most interested in initially was Fulton's seamless metal bellows. Invented
and patented by Weston Miller Fulton in 1904, the bellows were made
from precision-drawn tubes into which corrugations were formed. Prior
to his invention, manufacturing equipment capable of drawing a tube
that would meet precise engineering specifications was not available.
Consequently, Fulton not only had the bellows patented but also the

Punch press department. *Courtesy Jack Rouse.*

manufacturing techniques that were used to draw the required tubes. U.S. Patent no. 729,927 covered his device, which he called "Sylph" after a word created in the 1500s by Paracelsius, a German-Swiss scientist, that described mystical beings in the air. Fulton founded the Fulton Sylphon Company to manufacture the "Sylph."

Fulton, Tennessee's most prolific inventor, made good use of the technical education he received while earning his master's degree in mechanical engineering from the University of Tennessee. He was able to develop formulae that, when followed, would yield a bellows that had a repeatable spring rate, a known yield strength and a predictable number of cycles that it could be expected to attain. This new flexible device, often internally charged with a gas or liquid, immediately provided engineers with the item needed for making precision-type instruments such as thermostats, barometers and altimeters. In essence, this was the beginning of a totally new industry.

The company's unique capability was the reason the government panel was so interested in maintaining contact. For most of the bellows-related

Above: Fulton Sylphon plant, 1940s. *Courtesy Kelly Marsh.*

Left: Model holding bellows. *Private collection.*

items that the company was asked to make, the necessary manufacturing processes were already in place. For bellows and all of the other materiel the company produced, the biggest change was the volume required along with the requested expedited delivery times. This demand caused the number of employees to soon swell to more than four thousand. Three shifts worked seven days a week, with many employees often working double shifts of sixteen hours. This schedule became the norm for the next three years until the little valley helped to dramatically bring the war to a close.

The company often held all-hands rallies as it attempted to encourage its employees to buy war bonds. This, of course, helped finance the war effort—the same war that they were working so hard to help win. Movie stars and other entertainers routinely toured the country to promote the sales of bonds. One of Fulton Sylphon Company's rallies featured a popular singer of the time, Kate Smith, who to the delight of the large group of employees sang her iconic patriotic hit song "God Bless America." A thunderous ovation began as Ms. Smith's powerful voice belted out the last lines of Irving Berlin's famous tune to her audience of awestruck factory workers:

> *From the mountains to the prairies,*
> *To the oceans white with foam,*
> *God Bless America,*
> *My home sweet home.*

Same as others all across the nation, workers at the Fulton plant had rolled up their sleeves and gone to work. Many of these workers were inexperienced women and men considered too old to fight. By the end of the war, 8 million women were working in defense plants. Rosie the Riveter, with her sleeves rolled up showing her muscles and the resolve on her face, characterized this army of women workers. At the Fulton plant, in particular, the naval liaison officers with permanently assigned offices at the plant were stunned at the production of this mix of workers that extended from early 1942 until August 1945.

Every American bomber had more than one hundred bellows assemblies in its air frame and in the onboard instruments. The modern-day Fulton Bellows Company maintains in its archives the contributions made in the 1940s by its predecessor, the Fulton Sylphon Company. The partial list of materiel furnished to the army, navy and army air corps by the company follows:

Bellows for various uses	53,000,000
Hand grenade fuses	50,000,000
Shell boosters	44,000,000
Bellows assemblies for aircraft instruments	25,000,000
Other bellows assemblies	11,000,000
Five- inch diameter shell casings	11,000,000
Tail fin assemblies for 60 and 81 mm mortar shells	8,000,000
Engine thermostats for marine and land vehicles	3,000,000
Bellows for use in various instruments	2,500,000
20 mm steel shells	1,500,000

40 mm steel shells	500,000
Bomb fuses	325,000
100-pound practice bombs	300,000
Aneroid assemblies for oxygen regulators	250,000
Ventilation regulators for Navy and maritime ships	180,000
37 mm steel shells	150,000
1.1-inch magazines for cartridges	150,000
Barrel reflectors for machine guns	150,000
Bellows assemblies for 20,000 Norden bombsights (6 per)	120,000
Tail-fin assemblies for demolition bombs	100,000
Temperature regulators for war production processes	100,000
Detonator fuse bases	70,000
Manifold pressure indicators for aircraft engines	50,000
Control valves for Navy and Coast Guard Ships	40,000
Diesel controls for Navy ships	30,000
Cowl flap actuators for Army Air Corps and Navy aircraft	20,000
Part of shock absorber assembly for P-47 Thunderbolt landing gears	14,000
Air position indicators for carrier-based fighter planes	2,000

The following are not shown on Fulton Bellows Company's official list:

Bellows-sealed valves for the Manhattan Project (estimated)	5,000
Part of firing mechanism for 5-inch submarine guns (estimated)	500
Precision altitude detonation device for atomic bombs (1 per)	2

A company magazine advertisement during the war reflected the earned pride of a company that was doing so much for the defense of the country. The caption under a waving Army/Navy "E" flag read as follows:

Proudly we fly the coveted Army/Navy "E" flag with added star signifying continued compliance with requirements for over six months, presented to

THE FULTON SYLPHON COMPANY for high achievement in the production of war materials.

At the end of the war, the company received the Army/Navy "E" for excellence in performance award with five stars. This was the highest honor that could be awarded in the Industry Category. Each employee had earned the prestigious "E" medal for excellence and received it individually in a special ceremony sponsored by the Department of the Navy.

Work at the company, much of it secret, during the war years from 1942 through 1945 vividly brought to mind Winston Churchill's famous quote: "Never in the field of human conflict was so much owed by so many to so few." Indeed, after the war, it was learned that the company had been secretly helping an ally, Great Britain. Fulton Sylphon Company was the largest producer (more than 50 percent) of what the British called the computer unit for their own top-secret bombsight. In their version, seven bellows assemblies, rather than the six that were used in the American unit,

Proud employees with the "E" for excellence banner. *Private collection.*

were used to provide the alignment compensation for several variables such as rapidly changing altitude, wind drift and air speed.

The English bombsights were mainly used on bombers that went on nighttime raids or those that took part in pattern bombing missions. While it did not quite offer the accuracy of the American bombsight, Great Britain's military leaders thought that it offered them enough strategic advantages to consider its production vital to their country's national defense. This was demonstrated when representatives of the British military, always traveling in nondescript traditional business suits, often came to Knoxville and the Fulton Sylphon Company to confer on engineering issues and check the progress of their orders for bellows assemblies. Because of their distinctive British accents, and in an attempt to maintain complete secrecy, when traveling in this country they would avoid speaking any more than was absolutely necessary. Consequently, very few people, including those who worked at the Fulton plant, knew of the secret arrangement that continued until the war's end.

In the 1930s, Sperry Corporation, paralleling the efforts of Carl L. Norden Company, was also working with the War Department to develop an acceptable bombsight. Even though officials in the War Department did not regard it as highly as they did Norden's, they approved Sperry's version mainly because Norden was having difficulty meeting the government's large demands for his unit. Sperry furnished 5,563 bombsight-autopilot combinations that the U.S. Air Corps used almost exclusively on its B-24 Liberator bombers. Fulton Sylphon Company provided bellows assemblies for all of Sperry's requirements.

In perhaps an understatement, Fulton Syphon Company, and especially its metal bellows, had gone to war. A popular saying at that time was, "Fulton's bellows are an essential part of almost everything that rolls, floats, shoots or flies." Because of the secrecy involved, the Fulton employees were not immediately aware that two of the bellows they manufactured had played a large part in bringing the war to an end. They would later learn of the bellows applications on each of the atomic bombs.

After forty-five agonizingly long months, the war came to a sudden end. A few weeks later, President Roosevelt personally honored Weston Fulton, Tennessee's most prolific inventor, by presenting him with a "Certificate of Appreciation" for his war efforts. The president also pointed out the important contributions made by the company that Fulton founded.

For the weary nation, the end of fighting brought relief and spontaneous celebration. To show its appreciation for what the employees at the Fulton

Sylphon Company had accomplished on its behalf, the Navy Department sponsored a celebration as part of the award presentation when the company received its fifth star for its "E" for excellence banner.

Secrecy was no longer required, so members of the employees' families were invited to this large party, which was held inside the plant. For the party, the navy brought in some of the vehicles that had used the company's products during the war. On display as thousands of prideful employees and their family members walked among them were a dark-blue navy fighter plane with its wings folded up, a navy boat, a Jeep, a truck, a tank and several smaller items. Ironically, the party took place adjacent to the Press Department, with its heavy equipment that had produced 11 million five-inch shells for the navy.

In spite of the celebratory show put on by the navy and Fulton Sylphon Company, it would be upstaged by Carl Norden's company in Manhattan. Ever the promoter, Norden hired the Ringling Brothers Circus to entertain his employees and prospective military clients in Madison Square Garden.

CHAPTER 6

THE NORDEN BOMBSIGHT

By the 1930s, the design of aircraft had become sophisticated. From the materials used on its skin to the navigational instrumentation in its cockpit, the airplane was starting to resemble aircraft of today. Built by manufacturers like General Electric Company, Allison Company and Pratt & Whitney Company, its engines had become more powerful and much more reliable. Heating systems for flying at high altitudes were still a few years away, but some planes were being fitted with oxygen to enable the crews to fly upward of forty thousand feet.

For the U.S. Army Air Corps (now U.S. Air Force) in particular, however, there was still a pressing need. Its engineers and scientists had been searching for an accurate and dependable bombsight for years. With bombing run speeds of 220 to 250 miles per hour, knowing when and where to release the bombs was critical if the target was to be hit. Complicating matters, the bombs when released tended to follow the host plane at first before starting to start pitching down at a more vertical attitude. The trajectory of a falling bomb tends to make a geometric parabola. Making things more difficult, at the time no one was able to accurately calculate the trajectory of bombs that were often falling at speeds that were greater than the speed of sound, which is about 768 miles per hour at sea level.

When it became more and more likely that another war was coming, the army air corps pressed its search for a good bombsight even harder. With appropriated money to spend, it began working with several inventors who were working to come up with an acceptable bombsight.

Drawing tubes in the press department for use on Norden bombsights. *Courtesy Kelly Marsh.*

With an air corps contract in hand, Carl Norden, a Swiss inventor, returned in 1929 to Switzerland and lived in his mother's house while attempting to develop a more accurate bombsight. In 1930, he furnished several thousand of his improved bombsights to the air corps. The unit was better than nothing, but the army needed something better.

Left: Lady at work in engineering department. *Private collection.*

Below: Weston Fulton and U.S. Navy admiral Cluverius at the 1942 "E" award presentation. *Courtesy Jerry Riggs.*

Thinking that Norden was on the right track, the air corps funded more of Norden's development work.

In an effort to make his early bombsights more user-friendly for the bombardiers, Norden consulted with the engineers at the Fulton Sylphon Company in Knoxville, Tennessee. Thirty years before, Weston Fulton had invented the seamless metal bellows that were now in widespread use as the main element in many precision instruments such as altimeters and thermostats.

Norden used six of these bellows assemblies on each of his improved models. The bellows were engineered to expand and contract at a repeatable spring rate. With the flexible bellows providing compensation for such rapidly changing variables as altitude and airspeed, Norden and the Fulton Sylphon Company engineers, in essence, had developed an analog computer before the age of computers. This collaboration led to the development of the bombsight for which the army had been searching. From this time on, the air corps was much more likely to be able to release its bombs from a higher and safer altitude.

In the final run in to the target, the bomber often had to quickly try to dodge enemy fighter planes or flak. Norden's bombsight compensated for such rapidly changing parameters as air speed, altitude and wind drift. The bombsight would, in fact, become America's second-most guarded secret of the war. It was so highly classified and considered so important that army air corps personnel who were to be trained for its use had to take an oath of secrecy before they could even see one. The somber oath in its entirety follows:

> *Mindful of the secret trust about to be placed in me by my Commander in Chief, the President of the United States, by whose direction I have been chosen for bombardier training, and mindful of the fact that I am to become guardian of one of my country's most priceless military assets, the American bombsight, I do here, in the presence of Almighty God, swear by the bombardier's code of honor to keep inviolate the secrecy of any and all confidential information revealed to me, and further to uphold the honor and integrity of the Army Air Forces, if need be, with my life itself.*

In case a plane equipped with one of the American bombsights was shot down, to keep the device from falling into enemy hands, a thermite explosive was installed inside the sight. When detonated by a member of the flight crew, the heat from the resultant chemical reaction left only a molten mass. Initially, the navy had special floats on the wings of its Douglas Aircraft TBD Devastators so a stricken plane on the water surface would stay afloat a little longer to make it easier for the crew to escape. Early in the war, however, they had the flotation removed so these stricken planes would quickly take the bombsights to the bottom with them.

After a mission, a member of the flight crew on the air corps bombers could be seen carrying a sack when leaving the plane. The bombsight, itself never seen outside the plane, was promptly placed in a safe. This was often called the "Bomb Vault."

The bombardier entered in the air speed, altitude, wind direction and drift and ballistics data on the ordnance he was dropping. Once the target was identified, the bombardier would actually assume directional control of the aircraft through the bombsight, which was connected to the autopilot. Altitude and speed control remained with the pilot, but the bombardier controlled right and left directional control of the aircraft. Contrary to popular belief, the bombardier did not push a button and release the bombs. The Norden sight, using a system of internal sensing devices—including six of Fulton's invention, the seamless metal bellows and stabilizer controls—automatically released the bombs. The bombardier called out "bombs away" as the bombers lurched upward with the release of their heavy load. This rather primitive computer, although not primitive for the time, helped immeasurably in bringing the war to a close. With the successful development of the bombsight, the number of sorties that could be flown and the resultant collateral damage could be reduced in the war that was rapidly approaching. These calculations can now be easily accomplished using electronic technology that was not available in the 1930s and 1940s.

Albert Pardini wrote in his book *The Legendary Norden Bombsight*:

> *The Norden bombsight was born in the 1920s involving fundamental and applied research, such as an unprecedented bombsight engineering, design, complex mathematics, unheard of machining of metal parts to tolerances of in the range of one thousandth of an inch (0.001) to one or two ten thousandths of an inch (0.0002) on massed produced parts manufactured to watch-like measurements, development of precision anti-friction ball bearings, optical equipment refined to new tolerances, and the industrial ability to produce delicate instruments in mass quantities never before attempted. All of this was accomplished long before the discovery of high speed computers, calculators, and the event of the micro chip. This was a testimony to the ability of the American complex to react to a very critical time during the first part of WWII.*

Norden's bombsight had more than two thousand manufactured parts.

The government paid Carl Norden $8,800 each for the ninety thousand Mark XV bombsights his company manufactured. The Fulton Sylphon Company manufactured bellows assemblies for twenty thousand of these. Norden's profit was approximately 10 percent. The Carl L. Norden Company ranked forty-sixth among industries in the number of wartime contracts received during World War II.

Because of all the secret work being conducted at the Fulton Sylphon Company and at Norden's Manhattan assembly plant, security was especially tight. Photographs at the time show barbed wire–enclosed plants with highly trained and armed guards.

Incredibly, in spite of all of the heavy security, a member of the German spy network managed to steal the blueprints for the bombsight, one of the country's top secrets. A naturalized German immigrant, Hermann Lang, who was a member of the large and growing group of the New York spy network, had managed to get a job with Norden's Manhattan defense plant.

Lang worked late into the night as he copied the complex blueprints he stole during the day and took back to the factory each morning. His wife, who was already in bed, never suspected that her husband was committing espionage. After getting the job with Norden's company, he had worked at different times as a draftsman, machinist and assembly inspector. Each of these positions gave him easy access to the bombsight's top-secret drawings and specifications. No one at the factory suspected that the thirty-five-year-old worker was a traitor and a spy. His code name was Paul, and he was determined to steal the secret drawings. He was able to get the copied blueprints on board a ship that was bound for Germany.

At one point, Lang traveled to the Fatherland and gave the Nazis assembly instructions for the bombsight. While there, he was toasted as a hero by Luftwaffe chief Herman Goering and received a payment of $3,000 from the Third Reich.

Lang was eventually betrayed by a double agent and arrested by the FBI. He was tried along with eighteen other spies who entered a guilty plea. They were known as "the Nazi 19," and their trial was the largest espionage trial in the nation's history. Fourteen other spies who did not plead guilty were tried separately in Brooklyn, New York, and on December 13, 1941, were sentenced to a total of three hundred years in federal prison. The group was called the "Duquesne Spy Ring" by the FBI. Lang himself was convicted and sentenced to eighteen years in a federal penitentiary.

The double agent, William Sebold, was initially recruited by the Nazis to be a spy. The FBI was able to flip him to work for the bureau. With his assistance, the FBI operated a radio station for two years in New York City that enabled the U.S. government to listen in on messages that the Germans were sending to their spies. Also, the Germans never suspected that the misinformation that was constantly being fed to them from the radio station that they thought was being controlled by their agents was propaganda. The Nazi spy ring was the subject of a successful 1945 movie. *The House on 92nd Street* won an Academy Award in the category of best original motion picture story.

Ironically, except for the $3,000 in cash that Lang received from the Third Reich for the stolen blueprints, his efforts were for nothing. In spite of being in the possession of the plans for America's second-most important secret of the war, the Germans relied on their *Stuka* dive bombers and never used Norden's bombsight.

For America, the use of the bombsight did not end with the close of World War II. During the Korean conflict, the B-29 bombers were once again pressed into service along with their aging Norden bombsights. Then in Vietnam, about fifteen years later, the air force, still using some of the same bombers with their same complement of bombsights, was forced to recall some World War II technicians in order to make the bombsight operational once more.

With the advent of "smart bombs" and atomic weaponry, bombing techniques started changing rapidly, and America's bombsight largely became a relic and is now a much sought-after collector's item. The once treasured bombsight, invented by the Swiss scientist Carl Norden so long ago, was given its final assignment in 1967 with Naval Air Operations Squadron Sixty-Seven in Vietnam when they were used in Operation Igloo White to help with the placement of Air-Delivered Seismic Detectors along the Ho Chi Minh Trail.

CHAPTER 7

Volunteer Army Ammunition Plant

In the late 1930s, the United States found itself with too little capacity to produce enough trinitrotoluene (TNT) to be able to fight a modern war. Because of the specialized nature of manufacturing TNT, the producers of other types of explosives could not convert their processes to the manufacture of it. The Army Ordnance Department's answer to this problem was to create a unique entity.

The government would build explosive-making plants and have them operated by civilian contractors. This plan went into effect on August 1, 1941. Planning started immediately for the construction of one of these plants—the Volunteer Army Ammunition Plant in Chattanooga, Tennessee.

A few months earlier, the U.S. Army Corps of Engineers had evaluated the site for possible use. The location of facilities that produced high explosives in World War II had to meet the following basic criteria:

- protection from enemy bombardment by being located a minimum of two hundred miles from the coast and international borders
- sufficient availability of raw materials
- an adequate supply of labor
- a large tract of land that would allow adequate separation of facilities to serve as buffer zones for safety, as well as large enough to allow for future expansion

Maintenance employee. *Courtesy Chattanooga Public Library/Jeffrey Cash Photography.*

Acid storage tanks. *Courtesy Chattanooga Public Library/Jeffrey Cash Photography.*

- access to a main highway and rail facilities
- adequate electrical power
- ample water supply for the processing operations
- proximity to other ordnance plants requiring TNT
- potential for the plant to be built quickly

Having met these government requirements, 8,508 acres of land in Chattanooga were acquired in late summer of 1941. On August 1, 1941, the government retained Stone and Webster Engineering Corporation of New York City to design and build the plant. This firm was experienced in the construction of ordnance plants. Hercules Powder Company of Wilmington, Delaware, was chosen to operate the plant. It assisted Stone and Webster with construction and with the procurement of the necessary equipment.

Construction began on October 6, 1941, and by July 1942, TNT lines one and two were operating at full capacity. When completed in June 1943, Volunteer Army Ammunition Plant consisted of 433 buildings; 200 of these were room-size concrete bunkers with foot-thick concrete walls. Explosive storage areas were located to the east of the plant on rolling land that was not suited for manufacturing. Because of the shortage of steel, the processing buildings were made mostly of wood. The wood that was subject to chemical attack was covered with lead.

The plant was laid out in a manner that would lessen the likelihood that a fire could spread from building to building. The individual steps in the manufacturing process took place in separate buildings with suitable spacing between buildings. Workers wore "booties" over their shoes to negate the possibility of causing a spark. Chutes were placed in the walls for workers in the upper floors to jump through for quick exit from the processing area.

In manufacturing TNT, toluene, an organic chemical, was treated with nitric acid, which produced a crude form of TNT. It was then purified in a washing process using soda ash, sellite (a compound made by mixing soda ash with sulfur dioxide) and water. The finished product was dried and stored. Sulfuric acid was used as a dehydrating agent. The plant obtained toluene and soda ash from outside sources but produced nitric and sulfuric acids in-house.

Volunteer Army Ammunition Plant was a pioneer in the treatment of toxic wastes that were created by manufacturing processes. At previous TNT plants, the "red water" and the "yellow water" toxic wastes were simply dumped on the ground. Because of the proximity to Lake Chickamauga,

Left: "Miss TNT"—tops in war bond sales. *Courtesy Chattanooga Public Library/Jeffrey Cash Photography.*

Below: Displaying Army/Navy "E" for excellence banner. *Courtesy Chattanooga Public Library/Jeffrey Cash Photography.*

the source of drinking water for the Chattanooga area, this practice could not be allowed.

Stone and Webster Engineering Company was asked to build treatment plants. The red water treatment plant it built had an evaporator and an incinerator. The evaporator brought the water to a concentration of 35 percent solids. The remaining concentrate was sprayed into the incinerator for burning. The waste ash then fell into hoppers for disposal. Manufacturing stopped at the plant with the end of the war in August 1945.

Production resumed for both the Korean and Vietnam Wars. A Volkswagen automobile manufacturing plant is currently on the site.

CHAPTER 8

THE TENNESSEE VALLEY AUTHORITY

For more than a century, potential use of the Tennessee River was well known. Massive amounts of power could be generated, hundreds of miles of navigable waters were possible and flood-prone areas could be saved from annual floods. Rampant malaria might be eradicated, and thousands of jobs could possibly be created.

While potential was there, in reality very little had been done by the early 1930s. Many of the people who lived in the Valley of the Tennessee were in a very poor economic condition. Much of the land had been stripped of its cover, and rains eroded its nutrients away. Year after year, farmers tried to eke out a living from land that grew poorer with each crop.

With the coming of the Depression, the situation of millions in the rest of the country became similar to those in the Tennessee Valley. In an almost desperate atmosphere and wanting to jump-start the faltering economy, President Roosevelt and Congress remembered earlier reports from government surveyors that mentioned the vast potential offered by the Tennessee River. Therefore, East Tennessee became the first area to be focused on by Roosevelt's New Deal programs.

On May 18, 1933, just thirty-seven days after the start of the new administration, Congress passed a bill that created the Tennessee Valley Authority. On that same day, President Roosevelt signed the bill into law and said:

It should be charged with the broadest duty of planning for the proper use, conservation, and development of the natural resources of the Tennessee River drainage basin and its adjoining territory for the general social and economic welfare of the nation…Such use, if envisioned in its entirety, transcends mere power development. It touches and gives life to all forms of human concern… it will add to the comfort and happiness of hundreds of thousands of people and the incident benefits will reach the entire nation.

By the end of the first year, planning was underway for TVA's first big project: Norris Dam. Nebraska senator George Norris championed the TVA cause; because of this, the dam was named for him. The dam was completed in 1936. Several others were to soon follow. The total shorelines of the lakes created by the dams would eventually exceed ten thousand miles.

In 1933, only three out of one hundred East Tennesseans had electricity. Even when the dams started making electricity available, there were those who had little interest in acquiring it. In the first few months that electricity was available, its main use was to provide lights. Resisting residents often asked why they needed lights when their kerosene lamps were working fine.

Research on better fertilizers began immediately. The manufacture of better fertilizer was also started. A program was initiated that involved

TVA showing advantages of using fertilizer. *Courtesy Tennessee Valley Authority and National Archives.*

Home heated by TVA electricity. *Courtesy Tennessee Valley Authority.*

county extension agencies teaching farmers how to conserve their land and improve its fertility.

By the late 1930s, TVA's impact was being felt in a large and positive manner. Residents could flip a switch and turn on their lights or turn a knob and cook their meals. They could listen to their radio and not worry about their battery running low. For dairy farmers, electric milking machines meant the job of milking cows was much faster and required less manpower.

Industries across the nation began to notice the low electricity rates that were the result of the hydroelectric dams and began building plants in the Tennessee Valley. This was especially true of the defense-related plants that moved to the area just prior to the war and after it had started. Critically needed jobs were created.

Ironically, the same year that TVA was founded, evil and powerful people were emerging in disparate parts of the world. The Nazis and Adolf Hitler assumed the leadership of Germany, and in Japan, aggressive and militaristic leaders were also emerging.

As early as 1935, TVA chairman Arthur Morgan, in testimony before Congress, said, "An adequate supply of electric energy comes pretty close to being a matter of national defense." During the following six years, TVA embarked on a program that added a large amount of power-generating potential. Because of this foresight, the Federal Power Commission declared later that without TVA, the United States would not have been prepared to fight in 1941.

When war came, many TVA employees and contractors worked around the clock to build urgently needed dams and power plants. TVA had twelve major projects underway at one time. These projects employed twenty-eight thousand design and construction workers. With all of the added capacity, by the end of the war TVA had become America's largest electric power supplier.

TVA's Fontana Dam in North Carolina was a high-priority World War II project. The site was located in a remote part of the Appalachian Mountains. A railroad had to be built for hauling construction supplies to

TVA pouring concrete for another dam. *Courtesy Tennessee Valley Authority.*

Left: Watts Bar Dam project. *Courtesy Tennessee Valley Authority.*

Below: Night shift, Fontana Dam construction. *Courtesy Tennessee Valley Authority and National Archives.*

Norris Dam under construction. *Courtesy Tennessee Valley Authority.*

the site. A small amount of the wilderness was cleared, and dormitories, houses, trailers and tents provided housing for the workers. The little remote townsite soon boasted the following hints of a civilized world: a hospital, a bank, a library, a post office and a school. None of these had existed before.

Originally, power generated at the Fontana Dam was planned to go to the Aluminum Company of America in Alcoa, Tennessee. After a round-the-clock construction schedule, the dam was completed early in 1945. By that time, much of the power it generated was diverted to Oak Ridge to meet the demands of its uranium-enrichment program.

Working at maximum speed that would be difficult to match in modern times because of the large number of regulations required, TVA completed Douglas Dam and Cherokee Dam in an amazingly short time. Cherokee was finished in sixteen months, one full year ahead of schedule. Douglas was ready to generate power in twelve months and seventeen days.

In a joint effort, TVA and the U.S. Geological Survey worked together to develop advanced mapping techniques. In an agreement with the U.S. military during the war, this consortium made maps from aerial photographs of 500,000 square miles of foreign territory.

By 1945, a 650-mile-long, year-round navigable waterway between Paducah, Kentucky, and Knoxville, Tennessee, was completed. The managers of the newly arrived companies found the climate to be mild and

Prior to Fontana Dam construction. *Courtesy Tennessee Valley Authority.*

TVA construction equipment. *Courtesy Tennessee Valley Authority.*

TVA dam under construction. *Courtesy Tennessee Valley Authority.*

Above: TVA employees making maps of enemy territory for the military. *Courtesy Tennessee Valley Authority.*

Below, left: TVA poster. *Courtesy Tennessee Valley Authority and National Archives.*

Below, right: TVA construction worker. *Courtesy Tennessee Valley Authority.*

Opening of TVA's Douglas Dam. *Courtesy Tennessee Valley Authority.*

found that the newly formed lakes provided their employees with recreation opportunities. As the benefits the area was now offering increased, the companies began expanding the size of their plants, consequently needing more workers.

The head of TVA in 1944, a proud David E. Lilienthal, spoke of the future of TVA and America as he looked beyond the ongoing hostilities:

In the desperation of a fight to survive, miracles have been wrought in laboratories and with machines. Seeing the reality of things they had never dreamed could happen, men have been deeply stirred; now almost nothing seems impossible. Whether on the fighting fronts or tending the home sector, men are thinking of tomorrow, thinking of it with longing tinged with fear and uncertainty, livened with hopes for the future.

CHAPTER 9

Tennessee Eastman Chemical Company/Holston Ordnance Works

In the 1880s, George Eastman founded the Kodak Company. His company, located in Rochester, New York, manufactured cameras and photographic film. During World War I, the company was unable to acquire raw materials such as optical glass, gelatin, acetic acid, methanol and acetone from its suppliers in Germany. To prevent this serious problem from happening again, Eastman started looking to the forests in the Appalachian South for these resources, especially to those in East Tennessee.

Learning that Eastman Kodak Company was looking for land in the South, city officials of Kingsport, Tennessee, along with officials of the Clinchfield Railroad decided to recruit Mr. Eastman and his company. He agreed to visit the Kingsport area in 1920 and became convinced that the timber in the area would indeed be a reliable source for the raw materials he required, including the methanol and acetone the company used in large quantities.

Tennessee Eastman was incorporated on July 17, 1920, with $3.5 million in working capital. The company immediately purchased thirty-five acres from the federal government in Kingsport, Tennessee. Quickly following this acquisition, three hundred additional acres were bought for $1 million. The property already had sufficient available buildings to allow the company to soon start producing chemicals. Tennessee Eastman shipped its first batch of chemicals to its parent company at Kodak Park in Rochester, New York, in 1921. Its total sales for that year were $35,000.

Six years of litigation that had accused Eastman Kodak Company of attempting to establish a monopoly by acquiring other camera manufacturers ended in 1921. The company agreed to stop its quest to create a camera-manufacturing monopoly and concentrate on producing photographic chemicals that were needed by the other camera manufacturers. This greatly helped Tennessee Eastman since it was making all of the chemicals that would be marketed to others, and this led to several well-funded expansions. The big increase in employment made Tennessee Eastman Company one of the largest employers in East Tennessee.

In the 1920s, wood was used to make the methanol used in the manufacture of photographic film. Byproducts included charcoal, acetic acid and hardwood pitch. Tennessee Eastman expanded even more quickly when demand for film for home movies and for X-ray film increased dramatically.

Because of the extensive research that Tennessee Eastman's chemists had conducted, the company was able to produce acetic anhydride, another important ingredient in the manufacture of cellulose acetate. The company was now positioned to meet the ever-growing demand for its film.

The plant size increased again in 1930 when the company transferred its New Jersey hydroquinone production to Kingsport. In addition to the demand for film, the automobile and communications industries started demanding more of the company's newly developed molded plastic parts. By 1940, annual sales for Tennessee Eastman was about $29 million.

So, in 1941, when the world war started, the Tennessee Eastman Company was a profitable and flourishing enterprise with dozens of chemists on the payroll. America's War Production Board realized from the beginning of hostilities that much could be expected from that plant.

With the loss of the rubber plantations in the Pacific to the Japanese, the production of synthetic rubber was a top priority to supply badly needed material for tires for the military, farmers and civilians. The chief ingredient in the manufacture of synthetic rubber was hydroquinone, which Tennessee Eastman could be counted on to produce in large quantities.

Seeing the capabilities of the plant, its workers and its technical staff, the War Production Board asked the top managers at the plant to manage a separate government-owned plant at which the powerful explosive RDX (Research Development Explosive) could be manufactured. In 1942, at the southern end of Kingsport, a new plant called Holston Ordnance Works was constructed and immediately began producing large amounts of RDX for the military. The 425 buildings that constituted this plant spread across six thousand acres along the Holston River. When it was completed in 1944, the cost for the new facility totaled $77 million.

Left: Historical marker at Holston Ordnance Works. *Courtesy Holston Army Ammunition Plant.*

Below: Chemical laboratory at Holston Ordnance Works. *Courtesy Holston Army Ammunition Plant.*

The name of the new facility was later changed to Holston Defense. It would become the world's largest producer of high explosives. Because RDX was so sensitive, it had to be mixed with trinitrotoluene (TNT) to make it much more stable and safer to transport. This mixture was called Composition B. When used in depth charges or torpedoes, it was powerful enough to penetrate the hulls of German submarines.

At its peak during the war, the plant had seven thousand employees, of which 40 percent were women. The company's chemists had developed a continuous-flow process of producing RDX that enabled them to make it in large quantities. By the end of the war, the plant was producing 1.5 million pounds of explosives each day.

Like other East Tennessee industries, Holston Ordnance Works was awarded the coveted Army/Navy "E" award for excellence. Due in part to their feeling of patriotism and the belief that they were making a large contribution to the war effort, employee morale stayed high throughout the war. Interestingly, even though the workers were handling some of the most dangerous explosives on earth, only three died during the war years. These deaths were work-related accidents and not as a result of producing explosives.

As if Tennessee Eastman Company was not busy enough, as soon as General Leslie Groves was appointed by President Roosevelt to head the Manhattan Project, he asked Tennessee Eastman to be the first manager of the Oak Ridge site. After all, it was an expert in the field of explosives, and the atomic bomb was going to be the biggest explosion of them all. Management at the company thought they were chosen for the project partly because of their reputation of being a "get something done company."

Tennessee Eastman Chemical Company employees clock-in at Oak Ridge. *Courtesy Ed Westcott.*

Not knowing exactly why they were going and what they were to do when they got there, dozens of Tennessee Eastman chemists moved to Oak Ridge, which was one hundred miles southwest of Kingsport. It was early going, and the site was being called the made-up name of "Clinton Engineer Works" when they arrived. The installation would be named Oak Ridge later. With their background in chemistry, it is likely that they figured out the secret before others. There were, however, no reports of any type of public conjecture on their part.

During the war, the people of Kingsport bit their tongues and tolerated the influx of thousands of people who essentially arrived at the same time to work at Tennessee Eastman or Holston Ordnance Works. For the most part, the local citizens thought this was the patriotic thing to do. Even though the government attempted to control prices, the cost of items from groceries to automobiles invariably increased for the residents of the boomtown. To some, it appeared that the city and railroad leaders who long ago tried so hard to bring industry to the area had possibly done too good of a job.

CHAPTER 10

TENNESSEANS DURING THE WAR

Civilian

SECRETARY OF STATE

By December 7, 1941, Secretary of State Cordell Hull had been in several urgent meetings with his Japanese counterparts. As morning turned into afternoon in Washington, D.C., Hull was still engaged in talks that he assumed were peace discussions. This same Sunday had turned early morning in Hawaii. News quickly came to the mainland that the Japanese had attacked America's naval fleet and in so doing betrayed the hard-at-work secretary of state.

Long before the influential Tennessean had become President Roosevelt's secretary of state, he was a well-known congressman. He wrote the first Federal Income Tax bill and the Federal Inheritance Tax Law. He was widely recognized as an expert in fiscal policies. Hull was the main contributor in implementing the president's "Good Neighbor Policy" that involved twenty-one countries in the Western Hemisphere. He was elected to the U.S. Senate and served there for two years. Then, in 1933, President Roosevelt appointed him as his secretary of state.

In 1944, Hull was appointed to the War Refugee Board, which was established by Executive Order No. 9417. The aim of this board was to try and rescue the victims of enemy oppression, especially those who were in imminent danger of death. The Nazis' mass extermination of Jewish people was the biggest driver in this effort.

Hull and his State Department initiated plans for a future organization that would work to promote peace and cooperation among all nations. This organization would have military and economic power to help reach those lofty goals. Because of this work, the country lawyer from Tennessee was called the "Father of the United Nations" by President Roosevelt.

For the 1944 presidential elections, Hull was offered the opportunity to run as Roosevelt's vice president. His failing health forced him to turn down the offer, thus paving the way for Harry S Truman. Further citing health issues, Hull resigned as secretary of state after the 1944 elections.

In his *Memoirs of Cordell Hull* (1948), he wrote of his life and his long and illustrious career in politics. In explaining his vision of the future, he wrote, "I am convinced that the horizons of achievement still stretch before us like the unending plains. And no achievement can be higher than that of working in harmony with other nations so that the lash of war may be lifted from our backs and a peace of lasting friendship descend upon us."

CIVILIAN SUPPORT

The United Service Organization (USO) was formed in 1941 to provide morale and recreation opportunities for those in uniform. The USO, in turn, helped form the following organizations: Young Men's Christian Association, the Salvation Army, Young Women's Christian Association, National Jewish Welfare Board, National Catholic Community Service and the National Travelers Aid Association.

In addition to replacing millions of men in the nation's factories during the war, women by the thousands volunteered to work for the Red Cross

Learning to shoot.
Courtesy Jack Rouse.

and the USO. The enrollment in high schools and colleges dropped drastically as students dropped out to work in the factories. The Civil Air Patrol was established and depended on private citizens who were aircraft spotters, helped transport military equipment and participated in search-and-rescue missions.

Workers in defense-related industries were constantly reminded that their job was as important as that of the men and women fighting the enemy in distant lands. With the feeling that they were doing their patriotic part, workers agreed and put maximum effort in their daily jobs.

WAR BONDS

Initially they were called defense bonds, but after the attack on Pearl Harbor, the name of government-issued bonds was changed to war bonds. Americans were asked to buy these bonds as a way of financing the very expensive war that had just begun. They were indeed a loan to the government. The average annual income at that time was about $2,000, and the 134 million people were being asked to buy bonds regularly.

Bonds were bought at 75 percent of their face value in denominations that ranged from $25 to $10,000 and reached maturity in ten years. This meant that even though it was called "the greatest investment on earth," the buyers were paid back at a paltry annual rate of 2.9 percent. Ten-cent stamps could be bought and saved until a full bond could be purchased. The War Finance Committee and the War Advertising Council conducted the biggest advertising campaign to sell bonds the country had ever seen.

In spite of the very low interest return on their investment, Americans believed that it represented a moral and financial stake in the war effort. Advertisements were heard on the radio and read in the newspapers and magazines. More than $250 million in advertising money was donated by companies and private citizens during the first three years of the war.

War bonds became the ideal way for those on the homefront to contribute to the national defense. Rallies were held throughout the country in an effort to sell war bonds. They often featured stars like actresses Rita Hayworth, Greer Garson and Bette Davis, who in seven tours traveled to more than three hundred cities promoting bond sales. The "Stars Over America" bond tour, in which 337 stars took part, netted $838,540,000 in bond sales.

The government provided a promotional cardboard that had seventy-five slots for quarters. When full, this amounted to $18.75 and could be taken to

eat Tennessee in World War II

World War II bond booth at Oak Ridge's Jefferson Junior High School. *Courtesy Ed Westcott.*

a post office, where the purchaser would receive a $25.00 bond that would mature in ten years. Hotels and movie theaters helped to advertise bonds extensively, and most movies made during the war showed the war bond logo when the credits rolled at the end of the movie. These war bond logos can be seen today at the end of classic movies from that era.

There was a civilian "D-Day" in Chicago on June 6, 1944, when thousands of war bond advertising flyers drifted down from the city's skyscrapers in an effort to promote sales. The Girl Scouts participated when each scout bought a ten-cent stamp. These stamps were sent to their national organization, which purchased the bonds.

In 1941, Norman Rockwell painted a series of illustrations that was printed and circulated by the *Saturday Evening Post*. These paintings were often used on posters promoting the sale of bonds. These posters were a hit with a public that was interested in helping with the war effort in some way.

A few years previously, one of America's most prolific composers, Irving Berlin, had written "God Bless America." To suit the occasion, he now wrote

"Any Bonds Today?" This song, often sung by the popular Andrew Sisters, quickly became the theme song for the Treasury Department's National Defense Savings Program.

The Columbia Broadcasting System sponsored a nationwide sixteen-hour radio broadcast. Singer Kate Smith was the featured attraction and once again sang "God Bless America," her popular song at the time. The success of this show resulted in $40 million worth of bonds being sold to the listening audience.

Not to be outdone, professional baseball arranged a special game among the three teams that were based in New York City at the time. A ticket for this unusual game was the purchase of a war bond. The participating teams were the New York Yankees, the New York Giants and the Brooklyn Dodgers. Each of the teams was allowed to come to bat six times. No one paid much attention to the final score, which was Dodgers 5, Yankees 1 and the Giants 0. The United States government, however, was the big winner of the game, as it took in $56,500,000 in "ticket" sales.

By the end of the war, 85 million Americans, more than half of the population, had bought war bonds. Due to the government's massive efforts, it received from the sale of bonds a total of $185.7 billion.

RATIONING

In an attempt to save as many goods as possible for the service men and women, nearly all consumables were rationed. To implement the program, eight thousand ration offices were set up across the country. To buy an item, one paid in dollars along with the number of stamps required for a particular item. The following list shows the number of stamp points required for several different canned goods:

- Peas   16 points
- Spinach   11 points
- Pears   21 points
- Corn   14 points
- Tomatoes   16 points
- Pineapple Juice   32 points
- Green Beans   14 points
- Soup   6 points

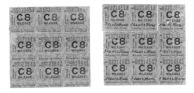

Sample of World War II ration stamps. *Private collection.*

Rubber and gasoline were the earliest items to be rationed. Ironically, it was not the shortage of gasoline, which was widely supposed at the time, that prompted this early gasoline rationing but a further attempt to limit the wear on tires. A critical rubber shortage was brought about because the Japanese had captured most of the rubber plantations in the South Pacific. Synthetic rubber, a poor substitute for natural rubber, was developed and used for domestic automobile tires. Nonetheless, the rubber shortage came close to being America's Achilles' heel. This worrisome weakness brought about a Congress-imposed national "Victory Speed" limit of thirty-five miles per hour. A little later, shoes, cheese, fish, butter, eggs, meat and sugar were rationed.

Color-coded and lettered windshield stickers indicated the amount of gas the occupant could purchase within a week. A black "A" sticker meant the driver could purchase four gallons of gas per week. The green "B" sticker indicated that the operator of the car was involved with work that was considered important to the war effort. Workers in the nation's defense plants with that sticker could purchase eight gallons per week. Truckers who were hauling supplies for the nation had a sticker with the letter "T" and were entitled to an unlimited amount of gasoline purchases.

On a motivational page in the 1943 Sears and Roebuck Company catalogue appeared the following appeal to farmers and ranchers:

You also serve—you who stand behind the plow, pledged to feed the soldier, the worker, the ally, and, with God's help, all the hungry victims of the war! You also serve—you who farm, you who pray and sacrifice. You'll feed the world even if it means plowing by lantern light, and harvesting by hand— even children's hands—even if it means putting up the trucks and going back to covered wagons once again. You're pioneers once more, with the best land on the globe to fight for—to keep free, and the best tools on earth with which to do the job. You also serve—and America salutes you—not for stars like a General's pinned on your shoulders—but for the stars you'll help keep in our flag and in the clean sky overhead!

SCRAP DRIVES

The government also encouraged civilian scrap drives. Nearly every consumable was in short supply, so many scrap items were collected. Rags were used by sailors to swab the decks of ships. Metal of all kinds could be melted down and used as material for bombs. Scrap paper was used as packing around equipment and weapons. Fats and oil left over from cooking could be used to make explosives. Scrap pieces of silk and nylon could be used to make the material in parachutes.

Schoolchildren were often seen taking tin cans to school in their red wagons. They had been instructed to cut out the bottoms and tops of the cans and place them inside the cans before mashing them flat. This saved space in transporting and storing the cans. Several schools had their gymnasiums more than half full of mashed-flat cans.

John Deere Company encouraged farmers to recycle their scraps in its slogan, "Sink a sub from your farm: Bring in your scrap." Popular actress Rita Hayworth toured the country promoting the idea of collecting and donating scrap material in a car with no bumpers and a sign that read, "Please Drive Carefully, My Bumpers are on the scrap heap." Because of industry's need for copper to support the war effort, in 1943 the U.S. Mint issued zinc-coated steel pennies. Much of the zinc was mined in Mascot, Tennessee, about fifteen miles east of Knoxville.

V-MAIL

Long before the advent of e-mail there was V-mail, or Victory mail. With millions of men and women spread out around the world, it was a daunting task for the various services to try to get mail to them from their loved ones back home. Even though mail at some remote locations was often a month or so old when it was received, it was always appreciated. In those days, the letter was the only way to communicate with those who were thousands of miles away.

The government developed a method of reducing letters into thumbnail-size microfilm reels. When the mailed reels reached their destination, the letters were enlarged back to their original size. The government encouraged the use of V-mail with promotional slogans like "V-Mail is SPEED MAIL." and "He's Sure to Get V***– MAIL." (Note the Morse code symbols dot-dot-dot-dash for *V*. The letter *V* always meant "Victory" and was used extensively in slogans during the war.)

The mailing public liked the V-mails because they usually reached their destinations much more quickly than regular mail. Government personnel liked them because of the volume of space saved on airplanes and ships. It was determined that 2,575 pounds of regular mail only weighed 45 pounds when sent by V-mail.

Rosie

Norman Rockwell's iconic 1943 painting of "Rosie the Riveter" was featured on the cover of the *Saturday Evening Post's* Memorial Day edition dated May 29, 1943. Rockwell managed to capture the spirit of the women who worked in the defense-related factories and shipyards at that time with its clear depiction of strength and resolve. Rockwell's painting expanded on the theme of "Rosie" from a song of that year that had been written by songwriters Redd Evans and John Jacob Loeb called "Rosie the Riveter." Even this tune was a takeoff on an earlier poster with the caption of "Winnie the Welder." One stanza from Evans and Loeb's very simple and compact song follows:

> *All the Day long,*
> *Whether rain or shine,*
> *She's a part of the assembly line,*
> *She's making history,*
> *Working for victory.*

A seated Rosie dressed in her work coveralls has a sandwich in her left hand, while her right arm is shown on top of her working-class lunchbox that is clearly labeled "Rosie." A rivet gun rests across her lap and her feet rest squarely on top of a copy of *Mein Kampf,* Adolf Hitler's manifesto. A waving American flag is shown boldly in the background.

Black-Out Drills

In East Tennessee cities such as Knoxville, Chattanooga and Kingsport, regular black-out drills were conducted. No lights could be detected through home and office windows. This was to make it more difficult for air raids by the enemy. Some people were able to have a very small light in a room when they placed a blanket on a window in addition to the closed curtains. Some got some light from the glowing embers of their fireplaces.

A certain number of siren blasts told the cities when to start the black-out, and later the sirens would sound the all-clear. Anyone not abiding by this rule could be arrested. Every neighborhood had an air-raid warden making sure that everyone was cooperating. An armband made the warden easily identifiable.

The Farmers

At the very time farmers were being asked to produce more food, their hired help was being drafted or was volunteering for service by the thousands. The problem became so acute that Congress added farmers to the list of those who held critically important jobs and qualified for a military deferment. To further help the farmers, Congress enacted an emergency price-support system that would stay in place for many years. The government supported a minimum price that the farmer would receive for his goods with taxpayer funds.

As they did so often in the war, women stepped up and did much of the necessary farm work. Children on the farms often did the work of adults. Several farm implement manufacturers decided to invest in designing and building equipment that would make the farmers more productive. They believed that with their technological advances less manual farm labor would be required.

Ford-Ferguson Company advertised that its new tractors could be used by "women, children, and old people to swell the ranks of farm labor." In another advertisement, it reported, "Here's the tractor that really helps women and children to do strong men's work."

Dempster Dumpster

Long before he became mayor of Knoxville, George Dempster invented the Dempster Dumpster. He held more than seventy patents that were related to the device. Soon Americans and many others in foreign countries were referring to all waste receptacles as "Dumpsters." This continues to this day.

Dumpsters were mounted on a truck and operated by one person. The truck backed up to a container that was loaded with refuse, and the container was picked up and hauled away. An empty container was left in its place. The Dumpster was manufactured by the hundreds of thousands on a twenty-seven-acre plot of land in North Knoxville. Shipping the heavy containers was made easier due to Southern Railway, whose property adjoined the Dempster Company's land, having a siding that ran along the Dempster property.

Nearly all of the major American military bases and those of several foreign countries used the Dumpsters. For instance, when the Japanese attacked Pearl Harbor, the navy had 125 Dempster Dumpsters located on its docks.

A later version of the Dumpster was called the Dempster Dumpmaster. In the days before computer modeling, Mr. Dempster would sit in his living room and make little models out of cardboard. Mrs. Dempster said that sometimes she thought her husband might be losing his mind. The Dumpmaster, however, was developed from these little hand-made models. With it, the operator pulled up to a trash container and, by way of controls in the truck, caused the Dumpmaster to pick up the container and lift it over the cab of the truck and empty it in the truck bed. The same container was then put back in place.

For several years, the welding expertise of the Dempster Brothers Company was widely known. Because of the company's reputation in this regard, the navy ordered and received fifteen thousand metal pontoons from the company during World War II. The pontoons were primarily used as flotation devices under the temporary docks that the army and navy built to move personnel and equipment inland in the areas they were taking from the enemy. Interestingly, the quality of the pontoons was such that the navy never had to reject a single pontoon.

Camel Manufacturing Company

Camel Manufacturing Company got its start during World War I when it made several thousand tents for the army. With the start of hostilities in World War II, the company was ready immediately to start making tents in large numbers. The company's experience in working with canvas and wax-coating of canvas led it to make myriad products for the military. In addition to several different types of tents, some of the products it made for the military included flight helmets, field caps, parachutes, leggings, Jeep tops, cartridge belts, cot covers, navy-style hammocks, motorcycle saddle bags, tarpaulins, canteen covers, sheaths for knives, mattress covers and parachute harnesses.

PATENT BUTTON COMPANY

America's largest manufacturer of metal military buttons, Waterbury Button Company, is headquartered in Waterbury, Connecticut. During the Civil War, the company provided metal buttons for the Northern and Southern troops. The colorful dress uniforms of several foreign countries sported brass buttons from this company, which is more than two hundred years old. The company also molded jewelry pieces and other civilian items. Early in 1942, the U.S. Congress passed a law that required all molding operations to be used in making parts for the defense industry. With all of button production coming from the molding process, the company was literally forced to switch to being a supplier for the military.

Prior to World War II, the Waterbury Button Company operated a subsidiary plant in Knoxville, Tennessee, that made a wide assortment of buttons to serve the many clothing manufacturers located in the Greater Knoxville area. Soon after the attack on Pearl Harbor, this plant, called Patent Button Company, joined its parent company in making metal buttons for the uniforms of all of the military services.

With metal of all kinds being in short supply, the U.S. government in 1942 experimented with a penny that was made of a type of plastic instead of conventional metal. The experiment focused on a plastic-like material called "Bakelite." Dr. Leo Baekeland had developed the material back in 1908 in his Yonkers, New York laboratory. In an article titled "The United States Experimental Cents of 1942," William G. Anderson wrote that the Bakelite Corporation of Bloomfield, New Jersey, "molded them from a plastic resin loaded with powdered metal to bring them to the weight of the one-cent piece."

The government paid for the necessary tooling at eight plastic companies and one glass firm so they could make the plastic coins as part of a grand experiment. Three of the eight chosen companies were located in East Tennessee.

The Blue Ridge Glass Corporation in Kingsport, Tennessee, was a producer of dark-brown glass that was used as part of an instrument that was used to detect counterfeit money. The government abruptly canceled its contract and announced that it was because the coins made at this factory were too brittle. It was learned later that the real reason for the order cancelation was because uranium oxide was being used to make a florescent glow under the instrument's ultraviolet light. The company's stockpile of uranium ore was quickly shipped to Oak Ridge to be used in the Manhattan Project.

Tennessee Eastman Chemical Company, also in Kingsport, and Patent Button Company in Knoxville were each allowed to finish its respective experimental orders. The finished strange-looking pennies were quickly rejected by the population in general, and the government deemed the experiment to be a failure. The coins continue to be highly sought after by serious coin collectors.

W.J. SAVAGE COMPANY

Knoxville's W.J. Savage Company held the first patent on an unusual-sounding device called a Nibbling Machine. The inventors were James Murrian, Kenneth Chapman and Weston Fulton. Their Nibbling Machine trims sheet metal, and some type of this machine is used today in every developed country. Murrian's initial description of the device in their patent application that was approved in 1939 follows:

> *This invention relates to nibbling machines and more particularly to that type of nibbling machines in which the punch carrying ram is reciprocated by an eccentric…From the accompanying figures it is apparent that my invention provides a novel nibbling machine having as one of its objects a new and improved stripper ring providing a shorter radius for the stripper with consequent reduction in the strain thereto; Another object of this invention is to provide a novel nibbling machine in which my novel stripper ring may be locked in any position through a 360 degrees rotation…A still further object of this invention is to provide a novel nibbling machine in which novel means are provided for progressively raising and lowering the ram.*

Evidently, U.S. Army personnel understood what all this meant and wanted several hundred of them. Their particular applications are not known. During the war, it is known that the company's sales increased by 300 percent.

JEFFERSON WOOLEN MILLS

During the war, South Knoxville's Jefferson Woolen Mills manufactured thirty-two-ounce Melton cloth. This heavy, smooth woolen fabric with short nap was used extensively in the manufacture of heavy coats for the military.

The famous navy pea coat, made of this material, is a good example of this product. Much of this material was shipped to Appalachian Mills, which was located about four miles away from Jefferson Woolen Mills. This major customer made heavy coats for both the army and the navy.

The cloth was named for a city in central England, and Jefferson Woolen Mills made several million yards of it under government contracts during the war. About 60 percent of the wool that was used came from domestic sources, with 40 percent from New Zealand and Australia. Nylon, Dacron and Orlon were minor components of the formula. Dupont furnished the dyes that were used in the dozens of stainless steel dyeing tanks.

The company employed more than three hundred workers and was able to produce forty-five thousand yards of cloth, requiring sixty thousand pounds of raw wool, per week.

Combustion Engineering Company

During the war, three thousand Liberty ships were built. They were never intended to be pretty and were often described as ugly ducklings. They were, however, reasonably priced and were capable of hauling cargoes of troops or materiel. Importantly, they could also be built quickly, some in as few as forty-two days.

The ships were 441 feet long and had a beam of 57 feet. They were staffed by a crew of forty-four and a contingent of twenty-five National Guardsmen. The ships were armed with a five-inch gun in the stern, a three-inch gun and two thirty-seven-millimeter guns in the bow and six twenty-millimeter machine guns at strategic locations.

The ship was powered by two oil boilers that powered a single-screw steam engine. This enabled the Liberty ship to make about eleven knots per hour. The six thousand boilers that were required for the ships were built by Combustion Engineering Company in Chattanooga, Tennessee.

Knoxville's eighteen-year-old Worth Campbell was on one of these ships as it plodded across the Pacific Ocean. The young soldier and several thousand other soldiers were gathering for the expected invasion of the Japanese homeland. While on the ship, Campbell was relieved to learn that the atomic bombs had been dropped over Japan and that the war was over.

SOUTHERN RAILWAY

Southern Railway trains on the north–south line and the east–west line crossed tracks in Knoxville. Coster Shop was a major repair facility located about two miles northwest of the center of Knoxville. About six miles to the east was the sprawling John Sevier Yards, where freight cars were sorted and put on the proper tracks and trains according to their destinations.

For shipping such items as tanks, trucks, Jeeps, petrol and all kinds of other materiel needed for the war effort, the train was the best option. Fast passenger trains also moved service men and women across the country to their assigned locations in reasonable comfort.

Southern Railway's passenger engine 1401 was assigned to the Greenville, South Carolina sector, but on occasion, it was loaned to other districts. It was one of several engines that pulled the train carrying President Roosevelt's body back to Washington, D.C., from Warm Springs, Georgia. So that each engine could be a part of history, each one pulled the train a short distance, fifty miles or so, and gave way to another engine.

Southern Railway's passenger engines had a distinctive color scheme. Green was the basic color, with gold trim and silver coated smoke-boxes. The colors were an exact duplicate of engines that operated on England's Southern Railway. Southern Railway's engine 1401 is now on permanent display in the Smithsonian Institution Museum of American History.

Southern Railway passenger engine 1401 on display at Smithsonian Institution. *Courtesy Allison and Andrew Whitener.*

This steam engine was typical of the big engines with high wheels that pulled twenty or so passenger cars along at speeds up to eighty miles per hour. Smithsonian curator John H. White Jr. described the colorful engines as "among the most celebrated passenger locomotives operated in the United States."

THE L&N RAILROAD

The L&N Railroad boasted that it had not had a single passenger fatality in twenty-seven years. This streak ended horribly on July 6, 1944. A fully loaded troop train derailed in High Cliff, a small village in East Tennessee, and four of the passenger train coaches landed in a ravine some fifty feet below the track in Clear River. A fifth coach was left hanging over the precipitous cliff. The coaches were piled on top of one another like match sticks. Thirty-five soldiers were killed, and ninety-one were injured.

The first responders to arrive on the scene were the mountain people who lived in the area. They used ropes, pulleys and homemade slings to hoist as many soldiers as possible from the wrecked coaches, which were lying in the bed of the shallow stream.

Every ambulance that could be located in the general area was dispatched to the wreck scene to take the victims and the deceased to area hospitals. The victims were taken either to hospitals in Jellico, Lafollette and Oak Ridge in Tennessee or to those in Williamsburg and Corbin, Kentucky. To take about fifty of the injured to the new hospital in Oak Ridge, which was about thirty-five miles to the southwest, an emergency train was formed when a locomotive was brought in and connected to the twelve coaches that had not wrecked and had stayed on the track.

The army's public relations group reported that Private Leonard Battag of Evanston, Illinois, was still pinned in the bottom of a wrecked car twelve hours after the crash. Private Battag, who had been in the army only thirteen days, was conscious and talked to his rescuers throughout his ordeal. Another soldier, in worse shape physically, received blood transfusions while being cut from the wreckage.

Acetylene torches were rushed to the scene to start the task of extricating those alive and the dead from their entrapment. An Army Military Police detachment and Company C of the Tennessee State Guard secured the scene and began patrolling the area to keep the large crowd of sightseers from hindering rescue efforts.

John Ruggles, who would later become industrial relations director at the Fulton Sylphon Company, was in charge of the FBI office in Knoxville and announced that the FBI was looking into the possibility of sabotage. A few days later, hearings were held by army investigators, and they theorized that the accident was likely caused by either excessive speed or a faulty rail. But no cause was ever definitely determined, and the army personnel soon went back to the business of fighting a war.

Like the managers of other companies, the top management at L&N had seen the real possibility that war would break out soon. In 1940 and 1941, the company scrapped large numbers of obsolete locomotives and freight cars, replacing them with 5,300 new freight cars, 14 steam freight locomotives, 12 diesel electric switchers and 8 new-technology diesel electric passenger locomotives.

The seating capacity of a large number of the cars was increased by adding extra tables in the dining cars and by eliminating lounge rooms in the passenger coaches. The number of ticket sellers was increased in offices that were located near large military bases and large terminals.

Additionally, bridges and trestles were strengthened. On many of their routes, heavier rail (132 pounds per foot) was installed. Several hundred spring switches were installed at key locations, which eliminated time-consuming stops and starts.

Due to the lack of business resulting from the Depression, several trainmasters had been furloughed. Many of these workers were called back to work as on-the-ground supervisors in an attempt to speed up operations. On some of the most important routes, special care was taken to build tracks that would support freight trains running at higher passenger train speed.

THE ARMY/NAVY "E" FOR EXCELLENCE AWARD

In an effort to encourage greater industrial production, the government introduced a new award for industry. Starting in July 1942, companies that qualified received a special award for excellence in production. Each of these qualifying companies received a triangular banner with a capital *E* within a yellow wreath of oak and laurel leaves on a divided red-and-blue background. The word *Army* was printed on the red background, and the word *Navy* was printed on the blue background. Individual employees received a corresponding small lapel pin.

"E" award presentation. *Courtesy Jerry Riggs.*

To qualify for the "E" for excellence award, companies had to meet the following criteria:

- superior quality and production standards
- ability to overcome production obstacles
- avoidance of work stoppages
- upholding of fair labor standards
- proper training of new employees
- maintenance of complete health and safety records

About 4 percent of American companies supplying materiel for the military received the "E" award. East Tennessee companies receiving the award included the Aluminum Company of America, Rohm and Haas Chemical Company, Fulton Sylphon Company, Tennessee Eastman Chemical Company, Holston Ordnance and the Volunteer Army Ammunition Plant.

Above: Receiving the personal "E" award pin. *Courtesy Aluminum Company of America.*

Below: Dignitaries at "E" award ceremony. *Courtesy Aluminum Company of America.*

Interestingly, one school received the award. Iowa State College (now Iowa State University) was recognized because its professor Dr. Harley Wilheim, working in the school's laboratories, invented the process of extracting and purifying uranium in the large quantities that were needed for the Manhattan Project.

District procurement officers recommended the plants to receive the award to the Commanding General of Material Command. These recommendations were accompanied with the reasons that those particular plants were chosen. The recommendations were reviewed by an Award Board. Companies that maintained their outstanding work record for six months after receiving the initial award were presented with a white star that could be added to their original pennant.

On the day the award was officially presented to the company, generally all employees were gathered at a single meeting place. Bands would often play patriotic songs, and dignitaries would speak. The individual awards would then be presented.

CHAPTER 11

TENNESSEANS DURING THE WAR

Military

USS *TENNESSEE*

In the first few seconds of the war, the battleship *Tennessee* was able to fire its guns against the Japanese attackers for only a few minutes before two bombs made its guns inoperable. Standing on battleship row beside the *Arizona*, the *Tennessee* was heavily damaged when that ship exploded. Wedged between the sunken *West Virginia* and harbor quays, it was ten days before the wounded ship could be freed.

By late 1942, the initial shock of the attack had been replaced by constant work. Many factories were now up and running at full speed. After several setbacks in the first few months of the war, the navy gave the nation a lift by winning its first big fight: the Battle of Midway. The outlook was looking better but still tenuous. It had become all too apparent that the conflict was going to last a long time.

The heavily damaged *Tennessee* was towed from Pearl Harbor to Puget Sound Naval Shipyard in Washington for lengthy repairs. East Tennesseans applauded when movie news reels announced that their namesake ship had returned to the fray on May 7, 1943.

Personal Stories

In 1941, Dana Allen, who lived in Knoxville, was a sixteen-year-old boy with an after-school job delivering telegrams for Western Union on his bicycle. A few weeks into the war, Allen and his bicycle started taking telegrams to families with the dreadful message from the War Department that they had been hoping and praying would never come. In 1943, Allen joined the navy and was promptly sent to the Pacific Theater. Even though he spent two years in the Pacific, he would always say that his previous job of delivering those awful Western Union telegrams was much tougher.

Joseph Messana was born on the Italian island of Sicily and moved to America with his parents when he was three years old. Shortly after his eighteenth birthday, he had the rare distinction of being drafted by both America and Italy. He elected to go with the Americans, who ordered him to England to prepare for the invasion of Hitler's heavily fortified Europe. On D-Day, Messana, now nineteen, piloted a small boat throughout the day hauling metal grating to be used to make roads for the Allied armies as they moved inland. After making a harrowing but successful initial trip through the exploding shells and bullets to the beach, he returned to his mother ship to be reloaded. This time, in the excitement of the moment, the ship's crewmen loaded his boat much too heavily, and when it rolled down the ship's ramp to the water, the boat kept going, directly to the bottom of the English Channel. Joe's life jacket supported him for five hours before one of the larger ships, which like the others had been busily firing its big guns, finally had time to pluck the solitary, and very cold, soldier from the sea.

Wymer George "Petie" Siler had served in World War I, but even though he was old enough at forty-seven to be father to most of the soldiers, he volunteered for service anyway. The graduate of Knox Central High School and a former assistant football coach at the University of Tennessee served with the 32nd Division in battles in New Guinea, North Africa and the Philippines.

South Knoxville's Sam Bowman spent his first night in Italy in a foxhole. The buddy assigned to him had a bandaged face with only one operational eye. Close enough to the Germans to be able to hear them talking, Sam asked his buddy if he wanted to nap while Sam stayed awake. His buddy replied, "No, I will stay awake, too. After all, three eyes are better than two!" A few days later, Bowman was severely injured and spent the next several months in many different hospitals. His family was notified that he was missing in action and presumed dead. After ten months of being sent from hospital to hospital, he finally made it to a medical facility in North Carolina. The staff there helped him place a call to his father, who worked in the Maintenance Department at the University of Tennessee. When Mr. Bowman was found and made it to the telephone, Sam said, "Dad, it's Sam." His father, afraid to get his hopes up, replied, "Sam who?"

Lafollette's J.V. Russell died on June 11, 1942, when his ship, the USS *Ingraham*, exploded after colliding with the USS *Chemung*. Russell's death was officially recorded as occurring on June 12, 1943, or a year and a day later. This was the military's policy at the time when a body was never recovered.

The patriotism that was being shown across America at the time is exemplified by the Davis family, who lived in Tellico Plains, Tennessee. The father, Hedrick, had served in World War I, and now four of his sons joined the army. A fifth son, Rex, was sixteen and too young to serve, but he would go to Korea a few years later. The sacrifices and hardships endured by members of the Davis family were recorded in the Congressional record by Tennessee congressman John Duncan on May 20, 2009. Excerpts from the congressman's speech on the House floor follow:

> *Madam Speaker, there is perhaps no greater sacrifice an American can make than serving their Country during a time of war, and no one can say the Davis family of Tellico Plains, Tennessee has not answered this call. It is a tradition that spans over 90 years.*
>
> *...Four of the Davis sons—Leonard, Dillard, Clarence, and Guy— joined the Armed Forces as soon as World War II began. All the brothers would fight for their Country and despite the loss of life in this great campaign, all would live to tell their tales.*
>
> *Dillard's story is one that took over fifty years to confirm. While on the Belgian Troop ship the* Leopoldville *crossing the English Channel on Christmas Eve (1944), a German submarine attacked, sinking the boat with a torpedo. In a series of calamities following the strike and a botched rescue, 763 American soldiers died. Dillard managed to survive and tell the story that the United States and Great Britain did not admit until the 1990s.*
>
> *...Madam Speaker, in closing, I would like to call the remarkable service of Private Hedrick Davis, Master Sgt. Leonard Davis, Staff Sgt. Dillard Davis, Cpl. Clarence Davis, Pfc. Guy Davis, and Cpl. Rex Davis to the attention of my colleagues and other readers of the Record.*

Most African American soldiers early in the war were not allowed to take part in combat operations. Henry Hastie, assistant to Secretary of War

Henry Stimson, decided that this rule needed to be changed. Hastie, an African American from Knoxville, Tennessee, led a successful effort that culminated in the decision to allow black soldiers to participate fully in combat operations.

EAST TENNESSEE PRISONER OF WAR CAMP

Most of the prisoner of war camps built in the United States were located in the South. The milder winters made the operational costs less, and there were plenty of remote areas. The military stressed the importance of the latter because they never ceased worrying about the possibility of sabotage at the defense plants.

Camp Crossville, a prisoner of war camp, was located near Crossville, Tennessee, on the Cumberland Plateau on a site that had formerly been occupied by a Civilian Conservation Corps work camp. Containing German and Italian prisoners, the first prisoners to arrive there were 1,500 German veterans of General Erwin Rommel's famed Afrika Corps. When America's ally, Great Britain, ran out of places to house prisoners, it asked the United States to take several thousand of its prisoners, many of whom were incarcerated at Camp Crossville.

Initially, the people who lived near the POW camps were apprehensive, fearing that the prisoners would try to escape and their lives might be in danger. After a few months, it became obvious that the prisoners had little interest in attempting to escape. Since it had taken them three to four weeks on a ship and a train to get to their POW camp, most of them realized that it would be too difficult to ever return home, and they reasoned that they were likely better off if they simply waited until the end of the war.

As was the case in most of the POW camps, these prisoners were given benevolent treatment. In general, the prisoners were cooperative, especially the Italians. Some worked for farmers in the area and received a small wage that was not usually as much as was paid to an American farmworker. A wage for work performed by a prisoner of war was mandated by the Geneva Convention. Others were forced to do work in and around the base. Those few who refused to work were often put on reduced rations. Sometimes, this would be nothing more than bread and water.

Surprisingly, security at this camp and many of the others was rather lax. For example, prisoners were allowed to go for walks outside the compound. During the war, there were 356,560 POWs in American camps, and 1,583 of these "escaped." By the time the war ended, only 22 had not been recaptured. One escapee from Camp Crossville who could speak fluent English was missing for several weeks. Eventually, he walked up to the front gate and was allowed back into the camp as if he had never been missing.

Abiding by the conditions of the Geneva Convention, the prisoners always had ample food and access to medical care. A newspaper printed by the prisoners was allowed. Those prisoners with no disciplinary issues could actually buy beer and wine out of their tiny wages. Educational programs were established, with English being the most popular course. The subjects of chemistry and mathematics were also offered. The prisoners at Camp Crossville could even take piano lessons from local piano teachers.

Evidently, the prisoners appreciated the treatment they received since many of them wrote letters back to the camps' workers soon after they had been released to return to Germany and Italy. Additionally, several former prisoners returned over the next few years for visits, and a few immigrated back to the area where they had been incarcerated.

The 117th Infantry Regiment

The National Guard's 117th Infantry Regiment was composed mainly of Tennesseans and was a part of the National Guard's 30th Division. The division's nickname was "Old Hickory," named in honor of the seventh president of the United States, Tennessee's Andrew Jackson. In September 1940, more than a year before the war started, the 30th Division had already been activated and was in training in Fort Jackson, South Carolina, which coincidentally was also named for the former president.

The division was moved to Fort Blanding near Starke, Florida, in October 1942. For the next several months, it lost its most highly trained officers and enlisted men to new divisions that were being organized for quick deployment overseas. After receiving replacements from other states and additional training at Camp Atterbury in Indiana, Camp Blanding in Florida and Camp Forrest in Tennessee, the division sailed for Europe on February 12, 1944.

The 30th moved into temporary barracks near the southern coast of England. As it went into further training, it was told that it was preparing for the invasion of the European continent, which was coming "at some point in the future."

On D-Day, June 6, 1944, part of the unit was dispatched to replace the heavy losses suffered by the soldiers of the 29th Infantry Division, which had been in the initial early morning assault on the beaches at Normandy. These soldiers were joined by the balance of the division between June 10 and June 15. The unit immediately went into battle with members of an experienced German army.

The main force facing the "Old Hickory Division" was the elite German 1st SS Division. When the 30th attacked a few days later in Operation Cobra, heavy casualties were inflicted on the German division, and this allowed General George Patton's Third Army to move forward and start his race across France.

After the shellacking by the 30th Division, Germany's 1st Division was reorganized and received reinforcements of soldiers and materiel. The two divisions met again in Belgium that winter in the large Ardennes-Alsace Offensive that later was called the Battle of the Bulge. There were several anxious days for the Americans until they recovered from the surprise all-out attack. Within about a month, the 30th was again on the move and mauled the German 1st Division so badly it never returned to battle as a unit. Due to the constant pressure the 30th kept on the German's 1st SS Division, the German High Command nicknamed the unit "Roosevelt's SS troops."

The division was the first unit to enter Belgium in October 1944 and was part of the force that breached the Siegfried Line and captured the city of Aachen, the first German city to be captured by the Allies during World War II.

The "Old Hickory Division" then made a rapid sweeping move that essentially encircled Germany's largest and most important industrial area, the "Ruhr Pocket." The city of Brunswick fell, and the division then captured Magdeburg, which lay along the Elbe River, on April 17, 1945.

Within a few days, the American army and the army of its Russian ally first met along the Elbe. The 30th Division occupied this sector for about six weeks until the area was turned over to the Russians. During this time, Adolf Hitler committed suicide and the Germans surrendered, ending the war in Europe. Because of its time on the battlefield and its many battles fought, the division was referred to as the "Workhorse of the Western Front."

After briefly occupying an area along the Czech border, the division was ordered back to the United States to prepare for deployment in the Pacific Theater. On the Liberty ships carrying them home, they heard the news that the atomic bombs had ended the war. They could stay home for good.

Private Harold G. Kiner was among those of the 30th Division's 117th Regiment who would not return home. For giving his life near Palenberg, Germany, on October 2, 1944, Private Kiner was awarded posthumously the nation's highest honor, the Congressional Medal of Honor. The army's citation dated June 23, 1945, read as follows:

> *With four men, he was leading in a frontal assault 2 October 1944, on a Siegfried Line pillbox near Palenberg, Germany. Machine gun fire from the strongly defended enemy position 25 yards away pinned down the attackers. The Germans threw hand grenades, one of which dropped between Private Kiner and two other men. With no hesitation, Private Kiner hurled himself upon the grenade, smothering the explosion. By his gallant action and voluntary sacrifice of his own life, he saved his two comrades from serious injury or death.*

The Army National Guard 30th Division had been on active duty constantly since 1940. The unit returned home on the *Queen Mary* and the USS *General Black* and was deactivated in Fort Jackson, South Carolina, on November 25, 1945.

The Longest Fighter Aircraft Mission

Because of the demands brought on by World War II, the minimum draft age was lowered to nineteen. During that same year, Jack Westbrook, who lives in Knoxville, reached nineteen years of age. Since he had never relished the idea of being a foot soldier, he decided to pursue the possibility of joining the U.S. Army Air Corps. Even though he had never been in an airplane, he was determined to be a pilot—a fighter pilot.

The year was 1942 when Jack passed the aviation cadet physical and academic tests. He still had a major obstacle to overcome—he did not meet the minimum weight requirement. For his height, he needed to weigh 128 pounds, or 5 more than he weighed. He solved this problem in ten days when he added three milkshakes and six bananas to his daily diet.

Because pilots were so desperately needed, the air corps relaxed its previous rule that mandated pilots have at least two years of college. This helped Jack clear another hurdle, as at that time he had only a high school education. In February 1943, he was ordered to report to Miami Beach for basic training that consisted of the normal saluting, push-ups and marching. After six weeks, he was sent to Davidson College for some training in mathematics and meteorology. While at Davidson, one of his physical training instructors was former University of Tennessee star football player Gene McEver. Jack thought it was interesting that McEver, even though he had a bad knee that was left over from his football days, could still outperform the cadets in every drill and distance run.

Flight training began in late July 1943. Jack's first lesson and his first trip in an airplane were in a Stearman PT-17, a biplane with an open cockpit. The next trainer he learned to fly was the Vultee BT-13, which was built in Nashville, Tennessee. Next in succession was the North American AT-6, with a six-hundred-horsepower Pratt & Whitney engine. With the end of training, Jack was commissioned as a second lieutenant and received his pilot's wings on April 15, 1944.

Two weeks after graduation, Jack was introduced to a state-of-the-art fighter plane: the P-40. This plane had a 1,150-horsepower Allison engine, and Jack became qualified to fly it with only ten hours of flight time. A few days later, he had his appendix removed and was held out of flying for three months. He then broke his nose playing in a pick-up basketball game and was held out of active service for another month.

After recuperating, Lieutenant Westbrook went to St. Petersburg, Florida, where he was introduced to the P-51 Mustang fighter plane. With a total of 444 flying hours, he was flying an airplane that was powered by a Rolls-Royce engine with 1,600 horsepower. His trip to the Pacific Theater took him through Nashville, Seattle, Hawaii, Guam and finally to Iwo Jima. He was assigned to the 506th Fighter Group on May 14, 1945.

Iwo Jima had been taken from the Japanese in February, and because it was relatively close to the Japanese mainland, it became strategically important. It was declared secure on March 16 at a cost of 4,600 American lives. Control of this island meant that the 506th and other fighter groups were now about six hundred miles away from Japan, and with their auxiliary tip tanks on each wing filled with 110 gallons of fuel, they were within fairly easy reach of the mainland of the enemy.

Retired colonel Jack Westbrook, 2015. *Private collection.*

The long and costly war the Japanese had been fighting had used up many of their resources, and gasoline was in short supply, consequently reducing the number of enemy fighter planes American pilots had to face. This enabled the American P-51s to do major damage to the ports and factories.

Some missions went well, and some did not. The following excerpts are taken from Lieutenant Westbrook's Mission Report dated July 28, 1945, and from his memory in a personal interview conducted on July 3, 2015:

> *For the first time the VIIth Fighter Command gave the green light for a fighter sweep. The mission was pure unadulterated rhubarb from beginning to end. The mission summary of havoc created was as follows: two locomotives destroyed and two others damaged; one truck destroyed and three others damaged; two oil cars burned; one "Tony" fighter plane probably destroyed; two seaplanes damaged; one lighthouse damaged; one radar station set afire; and factories, power lines, railroad yards and radio stations damaged. The report included the following notation: "Lt. Westbrook hugged the deck rather firmly and shot up several factories, power lines, a railroad trestle and a steel tower near the coast. In return, the enemy nicked his left wing."*
>
> *If the sweep against the Tokyo targets was pure, unadulterated rhubarb, the flight back to Iwo Jima was pure, unadulterated aerial frenzy. After forming up with our "mother hen" B-29s…we headed south. Within less than an hour, we were deep into a weather front with thunderstorms estimated to reach 30,000 feet…it became obvious that we could not fly through it. So, the B-29 navigators decided to… fly around the storm.*
>
> *As we attempted to avoid the storm…we at last found our way around it and headed once again for Iwo. The official record says we landed at 1641 hours, making a total flight time of 8 hours, 12 minutes. Notwithstanding the mission summary, this pilot's AF form 5 [flight record] reflects a flight of 8 hours, 45 minutes.*

If Lieutenant Westbrook's recorded time is correct, as he thinks it is, this length of time in the air would make this flight the longest fighter plane mission of World War II. His final combat mission was on August 10, 1945, five days before the end of the war, when his unit escorted B-29s on a raid against Tokyo.

MEDICINE MAN

Anderson County's Homer Stooksbury was working as an apprentice electrician at Oak Ridge's new Y-12 Plant when he received his draft notice. During his first few days in the army, he was given an aptitude test that indicated he would make a good medic. He started training as both a regular soldier and as a medic.

He was assigned to the 25th Division, which was temporarily stationed in Auckland, New Zealand. From there, the division was sent to Luzon, a Philippine island. In the regiment to which Homer was assigned, 60 of 260 survived the initial battle on the island. The medics were busy, and they would be busy for the next 164 days.

The 165 days of combat duty without a day off set the record in the Pacific Theater for days of continuous battle. Constantly answering the call for a medic, Homer went to the aid of soldier after soldier. For some he applied a tourniquet, for some he started an intravenous drip and for others he simply administered a shot of morphine.

Medic Homer Stooksbury, 1943. *Courtesy Homer Stooksbury.*

One night, Homer was pinned down while attending a soldier who had yelled that he was bleeding to death. He was forced to stay in a squatting position for eight hours while applying a tourniquet. Every slight movement of a foot made a little noise, and the bullets would immediately start flying. With morning light, he and the wounded soldier were rescued. For this act of bravery, he was awarded the Bronze Star. For the bullet wound in his hand, he would receive the Purple Heart.

A few weeks later, he dragged a severely wounded second lieutenant back to friendly lines even though bullets were dancing all around them. For this gallant action, Homer was awarded the Bronze Star Cluster. Perhaps that

Former medic Homer Stooksbury at home, 2015. *Private collection.*

aptitude test that he had taken a few years earlier that made a medic of him had been right all along.

All the time Homer was away, his mother cut clippings from the newspaper any time there was an article about Homer's Division, the 25th. She presented them to Homer when he arrived home in December 1945. When Homer arrived at his Clinton, Tennessee bus stop, an acquaintance told him, "I want to drive you home, because I want to see your mother's face when you walk through that door."

THEY ARE STILL COMING HOME

The *Knoxville News Sentinel* reported on July 1, 2015, that First Lieutenant Alexander Bonnyman was coming home at last from an unmarked, common grave on a Pacific island. Bonnyman's grandson Clay Bonnyman Evans and a team of researchers found and were able to identify the remains of his grandfather. Evans said, "I didn't count on this happening. When it did, I was shocked. I dropped my video camera and had tears in my eyes."

Alexander Bonnyman, who grew up in Knoxville, lost his life on the island of Tarawa in November 1943. Lieutenant Bonnyman led an assault on a Japanese bomb shelter. For his actions, he was posthumously awarded the prestigious Congressional Medal of Honor. After seventy-two years, Alexander Bonnyman rests at Highland Memorial Cemetery in west Knoxville.

CHAPTER 12

SPLITTING ATOMS

History records that the first person to call an atom an "atom" was the Greek philosopher Democritus, who lived between 460 BC and 370 BC. His description of atoms was amazingly similar to that of modern-day scientists. He thought that all things on earth were made up of atoms, which were indestructible, indivisible and in constant motion. He believed that their numbers were infinite and occurred in varying sizes and shapes. He reasoned that the strength of an item was determined by the shape of its atoms. He thought iron atoms would be strong with interconnecting hooks, while water atoms were likely slippery and air atoms would probably be weightless.

As with the theories of his Greek counterparts Aristotle and Socrates, Democritus had no way to prove his hypothesis regarding atoms. One can only imagine what would have happened if electricity and large magnets had been available during their time. As it was, centuries went by before history reports again on atom theorizing. Then as if a part of a large plan, several scientists started getting results in their laboratories that puzzled, excited and concerned them at the same time.

The ideas, discoveries and inventions of scientists and engineers around the world seem to spike a few years before and after the turn of the twentieth century. In 1908, Alfred Wilm introduced the aluminum alloy Duralim, and 1905 saw Albert Einstein introduce his theory of relativity. His simple-looking but profound formula of $e = mc^2$ (energy equals mass times the speed of light squared) would lead to his being called the father of physics.

At this time, several other physicists began to look at Einstein's work and were able to predict fairly accurately what lay ahead in their field. Especially in Germany and America, more and more scientists were becoming convinced that it was within the realm of possibility to split Democritus's atom.

As the group of scientists experimented and chronicled their findings, they found that the properties of several materials changed when irradiated. They puzzled over the radioactivity they were creating in their laboratories. To answer some of their intriguing questions, several scientists started working closely together. In addition to Einstein, this "Nuclear Group" consisted of Leo Szilard (Hungary), Pierre and Marie Curie (France), Ernest Rutherford (New Zealand), Hantaro Nagaoka (Japan), Otto Hahn (Germany) and Lise Meitner (Austria).

Rutherford, in 1908, observed that what he called the alpha particle was, in reality, an atom of helium. He followed this up in 1911 by stating that the nucleus of an atom is a concentrated mass surrounded by electrons in orbits.

Until the 1930s, the scientists still seemed to be creating more questions than answers, but this began to change when Adolf Hitler came to power; many of the alarmed Jewish scientists quickly moved to America. By sheer coincidence, Albert Einstein had been vacationing in America at the time and simply stayed. Some respected physicists such as John von Neumann, Theodore von Karman, Leo Szilard, Hans Bethe, Lise Meitner and Enrico Fermi joined him here.

Discoveries surrounding the possibility of splitting the atom were happening fast in the late 1930s and early 1940s, both in the United States and by scientists still living in Germany. The atom-splitting theory was becoming a real possibility. Each scientist realized the energy that would be unlocked if what they were seeing in their laboratories could be replicated on a larger scale. In this case, several were now certain that a bomb with an incredible amount of power could be produced.

The group of "in the know" scientists was now writing about such lofty subjects as fission of uranium atoms, starting a chain reaction, producing a massive atomic explosion and the calculations covering what they called "critical mass." This group agreed they were getting close to splitting the atom, which could lead to the development of a powerful new weapon. Because several of their articles appeared in scientific journals, scientists everywhere were at least somewhat knowledgeable of what was occurring.

Meanwhile, Japan, led by General Takeo Yasuda, director of Aviation Technology Research Institute of the Imperial Japanese Army, started studying the possibility of developing a nuclear bomb. He became intrigued in 1938 and 1939 after reading the scientific articles published in America and Germany that described the possibility of nuclear fission.

In 1940, Yasuda's aide, Lieutenant Colonel Suzuki, prepared a report that stated that Japan had access to enough uranium in Burma and Korea for them to develop a bomb. General Yasuda then assembled a group of Japanese physicists to discuss such a program. Several from this group had worked with nuclear scientists Neils Bohr and Ernest Lawrence. The following year, the Imperial Japanese Army launched a research program toward developing a nuclear bomb. Because of the war-induced strains on their economy, Japan's efforts were severely hampered.

Not to be outdone, the Soviet Union launched a program in 1939 with the goal of building an atomic bomb. This was after Igor Kurchatov, a leading Soviet physicist, alerted his government as to what was happening in other countries and the possible military ramifications. When Germany invaded Russia in June 1941, priorities had to be shifted and the project was reluctantly suspended. In early 1943, with the German military threat lessened, the Soviet scientists resumed their nuclear efforts.

The Nazis had determined that "heavy water" was a good medium to slow the speed of secondary neutrons, which was important in the splitting of an atom. When they invaded Norway, they quickly commandeered an operating heavy water plant in Vemork in southern Norway. After several unsuccessful attempts by British commandos and Norwegian guerrillas to destroy the plant, the U.S. 8th Air Force, on November 16, 1943, launched a raid using 143 B-17s, which resulted in the plant being put out of action. Not to be stopped, the Germans decided to salvage any working equipment and any heavy water they had already produced and move the entire operation to Germany. With the help of British intelligence, a team of three Norwegian saboteurs sank the ferry and its cargo on February 20, 1944, thereby largely destroying any threat that the Germans would be able to develop a nuclear weapon in time to affect the outcome of the war.

Leo Szilard, an emigrant from Hungary, realized the importance of the experiments taking place and likely being conducted simultaneously in Germany and other countries. Unknown to Szilard, German intelligence had learned of nuclear projects in America and Great Britain, and the Germans immediately put together a team to look into the feasibility of developing a bomb. Leading the German effort were three of their top physicists: Erich Bagge, Werner Heisenberg and Paul Harteck.

In 1939, Szilard thought it was of paramount importance that the president of the United States be made aware of the possibility that such a war-altering weapon could be built, and at the same time, their German counterparts were also close to developing a nuclear weapon. Szilard thought that since he was not well-known, the president would likely ignore any urgent messages he might send to the White House. With this in mind, he asked his friend, the famous physicist Albert Einstein, to sign letters that Szilard wrote.

Szilard wrote a series of four letters to the president. Each bore the signature of his friend Einstein. The fourth letter (in which "Einstein" was pleading for closer cooperation between members of Roosevelt's cabinet and the scientists involved in what would be called the Manhattan Project) was mailed only a few days before Roosevelt's death on April 12, 1945, and the president never had an opportunity to read it. Excerpts of Szilard's letters pleading for action by the federal government follow:

Albert Einstein
Old Grove Road
Nassau Point
Peconic, Long Island
August, 2nd, 1939

F.D. Roosevelt
President of the United States
White House
Washington, D.C.

Sir:
Some recent work by E. Fermi and L. Szilard, which has been communicated to me in manuscript, leads me to expect that the element uranium may be turned into a new and important source of energy in the immediate future...

In the course of the last four months, it has been made probable—through the work of Joliot in France as well as Fermi and Szilard in America that it may become possible to set up a nuclear chain reaction in a large mass of uranium, by which vast amounts of power and large quantities of new radium-like elements would be generated. A single bomb of this type, carried by boat and exploded in a port, might very well destroy the whole port together with some of the surrounding territory.

Sig.
Albert Einstein

March 7, 1940

President Roosevelt:

...Since the outbreak of the war, interest in uranium has intensified in Germany. I have now learned that research there is carried out in great secrecy and that it has been extended to another of the Kaiser Wilhelm Institutes, the Institute of Physics, under the leadership of C.F. von Weizsacker, who is working there on uranium in collaboration with the Institute of Chemistry. The former director was sent away on leave of absence, apparently for the duration of the war.

...Dr. Szilard has shown me the manuscript which he is sending to the Physics Review *in which he describes in detail a method of setting up a chain reaction in uranium. The papers will appear in print unless they are held up, and the question arises whether something ought to be done to withhold publication.*

I have discussed with Professor Wigner of Princeton University the situation in light of the information available. Dr. Szilard will let you have a memorandum informing you of the progress made since October last year so that you will be able to take such action as you think in the circumstances advisable...

Sig.
Albert Einstein

April 25, 1940

President Roosevelt:

...I am convinced as to the wisdom and the urgency of creating the conditions under which that and related work can be carried out with greater speed and on a larger scale than hitherto. I was interested in a suggestion made by Dr. Sachs that the Special Advisory Committee supply names of persons to serve as a board of trustees for a nonprofit organization which, with the approval of the government committee, could secure from government or private sources or both, the necessary funds for carrying out the work. Given such a framework and the necessary funds, it (the large-scale experiments and exploration of practical applications) could be carried out much faster than through a loose cooperation of university laboratories and government departments.

Sig.
Albert Einstein

March 25, 1945

President Roosevelt:
...In the summer of 1939 Dr. Szilard put before me his views concerning the potential importance of uranium for national defense. He was greatly disturbed by the potentialities involved and anxious that the United States government be advised of them as soon as possible. Dr. Szilard, who is one of the discoverers of the neutron emission of uranium on which all present work on uranium is based, described to me a specific system which he devised and which he thought would make it possible to set up a chain reaction in un-separated uranium in the immediate future. Having known him for over twenty years both from his scientific work and personally, I have much confidence in his judgment and it was on the basis of his judgment as well as my own that I took the liberty to approach you in connection with this subject. You responded to my letter dated August 2, 1939 by the appointment of a committee under the chairmanship of Dr. Briggs and thus started the Government's activity in this field.

The terms of secrecy under which Dr. Szilard is working at present do not permit him to give me information about his work; however, I understand that he is now greatly concerned about the lack of adequate contact between scientists who are doing this work and those members of your Cabinet who are responsible for formulating policy. In the circumstances I consider it my duty to give Mr. Szilard this introduction and I wish to express the hope that you will be able to give his presentation of the case your personal attention.

Very truly yours,
A. Einstein

Incredibly, the subterfuge by Szilard's first three letters directly led to America's acquisition of the atomic bomb. These letters that the president believed were coming from Albert Einstein were enough to convince him that something big was happening in the scientific world, especially regarding nuclear fission. At the same time, he was alarmed by the revelation that Germany, which was growing more hostile by the day, was almost certainly working on a similar project. Largely because of the letters bearing the signature of the world-famous Albert Einstein, a committee was formed of representatives from a broad spectrum of the government to look into the best way to compete with Germany and develop what the close-knit group of in-the-know scientists had started calling an "atomic bomb." The members of this select committee were urged to work in total secrecy and as quickly as possible. While Roosevelt and others now knew of Germany's efforts, they had no way of knowing the status of their enemy's program, which had been operating under strict secrecy for several months.

At this time, Senator Kenneth McKellar of Tennessee was chairman of the Senate Appropriations Committee. In this role, he was summoned to the White House regarding an important matter. He was briefed by Roosevelt about the work of the scientists and the committee that the president had recently appointed.

President Roosevelt explained that he was going to need an extremely large amount of money and that it must be somehow mingled among the other items in the budget and hidden away from the eyes of people in this country and abroad. Further, he indicated that a large, relatively remote tract of land would be required. Access to abundant electricity and water was also necessary.

Realizing the possible economic benefits from such a project, to Roosevelt's statement about the needed land, McKellar answered the president with a question. He half-jokingly asked, "Mr. President, in just what part of Tennessee would you like this plant to be located?" After all, a lot was being asked of Chairman McKellar, who was in control of the government's purse strings, and President Roosevelt knew it.

Concurrently, the pace of the project was accelerating among the teams of scientists who could see through their learned eyes that the goal of being able to create nuclear fission was close at hand. Enrico Fermi moved his team, which had been working at New York's Columbia University, to Chicago. There in a squash stadium on the campus of the University of Chicago, Fermi placed 6 tons of uranium and 250 tons of graphite (used as a moderator) in a "pile." On December 2, 1942, with forty-two observers present, Fermi's pile went "critical." For four and a half minutes, a self-sustaining nuclear reaction occurred. This action was stopped when the anti-reactivity rods were reapplied. This proved that the process could be controlled and that the project could continue.

CHAPTER 13

SECRET CITY

Oak Ridge, Tennessee

In September 1942, the Army Corps of Engineers' Colonel Leslie R. Groves was appointed to head the "Manhattan Project," which had been authorized by President Roosevelt in response to warnings from several prominent scientists that Germany was already working on a nuclear weapon. Groves was promptly promoted to general. His first decision was to construct a plant in Tennessee in an area known as Black Oak Ridge, where isotope separation producing U-235 from U-238 in sufficient volume to make atomic weapons would occur. At the same time, Groves chose Hanford, Washington, as the site for producing plutonium, which would be the fuel for another type of nuclear weapon.

General Groves found that the remote East Tennessee location met many of his requirements. Abundant water from the Clinch River was nearby. The roads were adequate, and a good rail line was already in place. TVA was in position to supply the massive amount of electricity that would be required. If this were not enough, the land could be acquired cheaply. The relatively small number of families living in the area, although it was a heartbreaking experience for them, could be relocated easily by the army. Ironically, a few of the families being moved had been relocated by TVA a few years earlier when it built Norris Dam, the first of its dams.

Land acquisition started immediately. Some residents found out that the government was taking their land only when they read a notice that had been nailed to a front fence post. Some fought the process, but all lost. A year later, they had been moved from farms and small villages that had names such as Wheat, Scarboro, Elza and Robertsville. One-eighth of Roane County and one-seventh of Anderson County made up the reservation, which was seventeen miles long and averaged seven miles in width and encompassed fifty-nine thousand acres. Groves chose "Oak Ridge" for the name of the site, even though there never had been a place called Oak Ridge. It would rise from the dirt and mud of open fields.

From the outset, security was a concern. The Clinch River meandered around the site on three sides and helped provide good security. A fence was built to cover the entire northern side.

An Auxiliary Military policewoman. *Courtesy Ed Westcott.*

Armed guards were at the gates and on constant patrol. Everyone wishing to enter the facility was told that they must have a badge and a purpose to gain entry. There was an attempt to separate the scientists and engineers working on different projects so they would not be as likely to discuss their work. Secrecy was so complete that when potential workers first arrived in Knoxville, the largest nearby city, and asked taxi drivers to take them to Oak Ridge for a job interview, they were met by blank stares.

In spite of the tight security, scientists from Germany, Italy and other European countries were added to the growing pool of scientists. Several soldiers with technical training were reassigned to work essentially as civilians at the site. The military unit assigned to the reservation was from the Army Corps of Engineers. Later, two companies of WACs joined them.

Young women from across America, often those who had just graduated from high school, were hired by the thousands to operate the equipment that controlled the uranium enrichment process. As they turned knobs as instructed, none knew what was happening behind her instrument panel. Interestingly, their production rate was superior to scientists and engineers who were tried at the same task. The reason given for this was they wasted no time questioning what they were doing. Other women filled positions vacated by men in the military. Still others served in the Army Auxiliary.

Keeping secrets—Oak Ridge's message to workers. *Courtesy Y-12 National Security Complex Photographic Archives.*

First graphite reactor. *Courtesy Y-12 National Security Complex Photographic Archives.*

With so many scientists, engineers and other workers arriving daily, great effort was made to somehow keep them and their families content in this remote area. A town was laid out that was near, but separate from, the plants being constructed. Streets were named for the various states and were in alphabetical order. Any side street that branched off these main streets carried the first letter of the main street. This system was adopted to help the new residents find their way around town. By 1945, the number of workers on the Oak Ridge reservation had reached eighty thousand, making the city the fifth largest in Tennessee in only two years. Reliance on traveling on the reservation by bus led to Oak Ridge having the nation's sixth-largest bus operation.

For several months, obtaining sufficient housing was a major problem. The early houses, which were constructed using a mixture of bonded cement and asbestos called Cemesto, could not be built fast enough, so hundreds of apartments and dormitories were built. Yet this was not enough, and trailers, hutments, barracks and plywood flat-top houses started appearing on the ridges and in the valleys.

Brazing ends of a bellows-sealed valve. *Courtesy Y-12 National Security Complex Photographic Archives.*

Above: Shift change at Y-12 Plant. *Courtesy Y-12 National Security Complex Photographic Archives.*

Right: Girl Scouts outside X-10 Plant. *Courtesy Y-12 National Security Complex Photographic Archives.*

In the interest of helping win the war, Oak Ridge residents endured hardships that often involved outdoor facilities and poorly heated houses. Eventually, libraries, grocery stores and even department stores would come, but those were still months away. The workers and their families put up with the gritty dust that collected between their teeth or, alternatively, the mud that often enveloped their boots. The workers felt that all of the sacrifices would be worth it if total victory could be achieved—a victory in which they could be proud of the major role they played.

While a town that had never existed was being built, Groves oversaw the construction of three gigantic plants to accomplish the major objective of the operation. The reservation consisted of three major plants—X-10, Y-12 and K-25—and served as the nation's headquarters for all of the activity surrounding the Manhattan Project.

Groves decided that the plants in Oak Ridge would pursue two main methods of enriching uranium. The electromagnetic method used massive magnets to separate the lighter U-235 from the heavier U-238. The gaseous diffusion process used porous barriers through which uranium hexafluoride gas was pumped. The lighter U-235 molecules passed through the barriers easier than the molecules of U-238. The U-235 was collected by using a chemical process.

Muddy street, early Oak Ridge. *Courtesy Y-12 National Security Complex Photographic Archives.*

General Groves, Manhattan project manager. *Courtesy Y-12 National Security Complex Photographic Archives.*

A third method of uranium enrichment was short-lived but became a part of the Manhattan Project's history. In 1944, the world's largest power plant that was to be used by the gaseous diffusion plant was finished, but the needed barriers that would make the plant itself operational had not yet been perfected. While waiting impatiently, Groves received a letter from noted physicist Robert Oppenheimer that informed him that the navy had quietly been enriching uranium for use on submarines by a process called thermal diffusion. Oppenheimer pointed out that if this process were used, the already-finished power plant could furnish the required heat for the thermal diffusion method. Within a month, Oak Ridge's S-50 plant was under construction.

The stop-gap plant operated for only three months. The slightly enriched uranium it produced was sent to the plant that was enriching by the electromagnetic method. This small contribution was said to have shortened the war by about three weeks.

Each of these processes presented unique problems. The electromagnetic method, using gigantic magnets, required vast amounts of copper at a time when, because of the war requirements, there was a nationwide shortage of copper. Groves and his team determined that silver could be substituted for copper. Colonel Ken Nichols was dispatched by train to West Point, New York, where the Treasury Department stockpiled America's silver.

When told that he would need thousands of tons of silver, managers at the Treasury Department were startled and told Nichols that around there they only talked of Troy ounces. Nichols and his assistants went into another room and did some quick calculations. When they returned, Nichols told them, "OK, we need 330 million Troy ounces of silver." This equated to fourteen thousand tons of silver, which was hastily shipped to the Manhattan Project in Oak Ridge, Tennessee.

Another hurdle was the need to acquire uranium ore in sufficient amounts to make bombs. It was known that since 1915, the Shinkolobwe mines in the Katanga Province of the Democratic Republic of the Congo had been yielding high-grade uranium ore. The government searchers were surprised and elated to find that a company led by Edgar Sengier, director of Union Miniere du Haut Katanga on Staten Island in New York, had accumulated 1,200 tons of uranium ore and had it stored in a warehouse on Long Island. Additionally, the company had 3,000 tons of ore stored at the mine site in Africa. All of this ore was purchased by the government's Colonel Ken Nichols. Later, Nichols would say:

> Our best source, the Shinkolobwe mine, represented a freak occurrence in nature. It contained a highly rich lode of uranium pitchblende. Nothing like it has ever again been found. The ore already in the United States contained 65 percent U_3O_8, while the pitchblende aboveground in the Congo amounted to a thousand tons of 65 percent ore, and the waste piles of ore contained two thousand tons of 20 percent U_3O_8. To illustrate the uniqueness of Sengier's stockpile, after the war the MED and the AEC considered ore containing three-tenths of 1 percent as a good find. Without Sengier's foresight in stockpiling ore in the United States and aboveground in Africa, we simply would not have had the amounts of uranium needed to justify building the large separation plants and the plutonium reactors.

The U.S. Army Corps of Engineers dispatched a team to Leopoldville in the Congo to enlarge the river port there and to build a more modern airport. Between 1942 and 1944, the U.S. government bought from the owners of the mine about thirty thousand tons of uranium ore. The importance of this site necessitated unusually heavy security measures. As a security precaution, the location of the mine was removed from all maps. Journalists were given no information and were denied access to the mine.

Work on the X-10 plant began in February 1943. This plant explored methods for creating plutonium, a new fissionable element. Once the production means were worked out, a site at Hanford, Washington, began the main production of plutonium.

Construction on the Y-12 plant got underway in the spring of 1943, with Tennessee Eastman Company as the operator of the site. Its mission was to separate as much uranium-235 from uranium-238 as possible in a short time using the electromagnetic method.

Early construction at Y-12 plant. *Courtesy Y-12 National Security Complex Photographic Archives.*

Above: Example of electromagnetic track for enriching uranium. *Courtesy Y-12 National Security Complex Photographic Archives.*

Below: Calutrons-controlled uranium enrichment process. *Courtesy Y-12 National Security Complex Photographic Archives.*

End of war celebration. *Courtesy Y-12 National Security Complex Photographic Archives.*

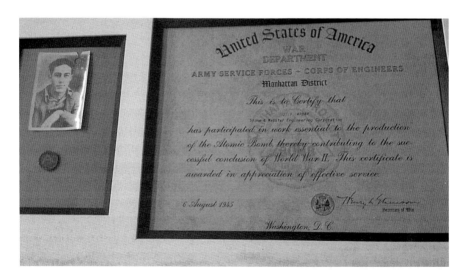

"A" award for those who worked on the Manhattan Project. *Courtesy Clara Arban Murphy.*

Building got underway at the K-25 plant in the fall of 1943. Here, the goal was to enrich uranium using the gaseous diffusion process. In this method, uranium hexafluoride gas was repeatedly passed through membranes, which allowed the slightly lighter U-235 isotopes to become concentrated.

Work at the three plants progressed smoothly and essentially stayed on the schedule that General Groves had laid out for them. So, in 1945, the tiny amount of enriched uranium that the two massive plants had been able to gather was shipped to a newly constructed Manhattan Project site in Los Alamos, New Mexico. Under the leadership of Dr. J. Robert Oppenheimer, the enriched uranium became the core of the first atomic bomb, called "Little Boy." A few days later, plutonium from the Hanford site arrived in Los Alamos. It became the heart of the second bomb, "Fat Man." Only after the bombs were dropped did the Oak Ridge workers realize the importance of the jobs they had been doing—work that helped bring the war to a sudden and dramatic end.

CORRESPONDING WITH MARGARET MEAD

Realizing that such a city had never before been built, the well-known anthropologist Margaret Mead became interested in how the thousands of inhabitants handled the stress of being away from home, having no idea what their work was accomplishing and living inside barbed wire–topped fences in little cramped preformed hutments.

By happanstance, Mrs. Mead had met and become friends with Connecticut-born Thelma Present at New York's Columbia University several years previously. Upon learning that Mrs. Present would be moving with her nuclear physicist husband, Richard, to Oak Ridge, Mrs. Mead requested that Thelma interview as many early Oak Ridgers as possible and report the results of these interviews by mail. Margaret Mead's "private correspondent" would eventually write dozens of letters as she described the citizens of "this strange land." Thelma seemed to be intrigued by her life in Oak Ridge and her participation in a "fascinating and unparalleled experiment."

The large volume of correspondence between Thelma and Margaret Mead was sufficient to enable Thelma to chronicle their exchange of messages in an interesting and informative book that was published by the East Tennessee Historical Society in 1985. Her book is entitled *Dear Margaret*, and excerpts of a few of Thelma's reports follow.

In an interview with Ann Wachter, Thelma was told that in the early days of Oak Ridge she had been noticing that her bus had started stopping at unfamiliar places. Further, she said that she saw "loads and loads of bathtubs…I thought, 'What in the world!'" Ann indicated that there was always an abundance of rumors and wild tales about what was going on in *that* place.

Laffitte Howard, head of the Associated Press Bureau in Knoxville, reported that in the early '40s, "all mention of splitting an atom…had vanished from the newspapers, magazines, and scientific works available to the public." Further, he said that he noticed that scientists from the universities who had been experimenting with the splitting of atoms started gathering in Knoxville.

Helen Jernigan described Oak Ridge in 1944: "It was a very lively place. There were no nights there. There were bright lights and loudspeakers on high poles…It was an adventuresome place, a boom town." She remembered that a large number of American Indian construction workers brought in from Oklahoma were on the site and that they were constantly "teasing the girls…and war whooping." She said that in fun they would pretend to be scalping the girls and that in general the Indians "put on a great show."

Ida Coveyou said that she knew a man who ran a clothing store in New York City. One day, he received a large order for ladies' undergarments from Oak Ridge, Tennessee. After inquiring, he learned that only seventy-five people were supposed to be living there. When he received another big order three weeks later, he became suspicious. He started thinking, "My God, they're running a prostitution center for soldiers or sailors there. Or something like that."

"By the fall of '44 some East Tennesseans were near revolt," reported Lafitte Howard. The area businesses were already suffering labor shortages because of the demands of the war effort, and now the "mystery city" was luring away even more employees. In an effort to smooth relations with the area business leaders, General Leslie Groves invited more than one hundred of them, including Howard, to join him for a tour of the reservation and a fine dinner. "The General moved among us, chatting… and seeing highball glasses were kept filled. Then dinner—thick steaks, a rarity for all in those meat-rationed times." After dinner, Groves told the group that the inconvenience and sacrifices they were making would be well worth it. Howard indicated that after that night, the relations with the Secret City's neighbors were much improved "and stayed that way until the bomb fell."

Kathryn Cantrell told Thelma Present that she had known a young lady who was shocked when she first moved to the reservation. She said that the lady noted, "The mail will never find me here. I am at the end of civilization." About a year later, when the young lady went to the hospital to deliver a baby, she was welcomed by a nurse who said, "Oh no! Not another one!" Thirteen babies had been born on the nurse's shift. While at the hospital, the new mother learned that the beleaguered General Groves often spent nights in the maternity room of the hospital so no one would be able to find him.

Clifford Seeber knew of only one person who took the secret seriously enough to quit his job in protest. He thought the government was wasting too much money. "I don't care what it is, from the money they are spending to make it, I know it would be cheaper for the government to buy it already made."

In Thelma Present's final and rather melancholy letter to her longtime friend Margaret Mead, she wrote:

> *The honeymoon is over. It was nice while it lasted. Was Oak Ridge's coming of age spoiled by the emergence from slacks and muddy shoes to more sophisticated apparel, by transition from boardwalks to paved roads, to neon lights, motels, fast-food chains, and the usual trappings of our more usual cities? By these standards, I suppose one could call Oak Ridge a "normal" city today.*

CHAPTER 14

SECRET LETTERS PERTAINING TO THE NUCLEAR FISSION RACE WITH GERMANY

By 1942, plans for creating a bomb as part of the Manhattan Project were progressing reasonably well. Even though America's top nuclear physicists were aware that the project was on schedule, they were deeply worried. They knew full well that their counterparts in Germany, with whom they were personally acquainted, were working on a similar project. They had no way of knowing the status of the Nazis' program, but they felt sure that if the Germans obtained such a weapon first, America would be in grave peril. The following excerpts from reconstructed and now declassified letters show their deep concern and seem to indicate that somehow they were generally aware of the happenings in Germany. At the top of each letter, the word "SECRET" was stamped.

The University of Chicago
Metallurgical Laboratory

June 22, 1942
Dr. Vannevar Bush
Washington, DC

Dear Van:

We have recently become aware that the threat of German fission bombs is even more imminent than we supposed... This is because we have just recognized how a chain reaction started with a small heavy water plant, can quickly supply material for a high power plant for producing "copper." If the Germans know what we know—and we dare not discount their knowledge—they should be dropping fission bombs on us in 1945, a year before our bombs are planned to be ready.

The exceedingly serious picture thus presented is, I fear, all too probably true. If it is correct, what can we do to escape defeat? There are, I believe, only three chances:

- *Complete domination of Germany before about June, 1945.*
- *Destruction of their fission plants by sabotage, air, or commando forces.*
- *Speed our schedule to beat theirs.*

Clearly none of these proposals is an easy one. My view is that destructive raids combined with all possible speed in our own development is the most hopeful plan…The bombs [those of the Germans] *can be expected to be ready in 444 to 650 days after the first of September 1941…The above estimates imply, of course, that they are looking ahead to their further needs to a much greater extent than we are doing, so far, and they are willing to build plants for not yet existing materials and extraction plants for the production of these plants, well before they have started to operate. It also involves the assumption that they are doing research on the chemical problems and on the efficient use of 49* [likely code for uranium used by Manhattan Project scientists] *much before these problems actually arise. This procedure involves a certain loss of efficiency in the use of personnel and material, which they would sacrifice in the interests of speed.*

P.S. My own estimate of the minimum possible time agrees with that of Wigner, but considering the inevitable delays that will occur in such a new development, I should place "a most probable" date for completion of their work as about November, 1943.

A.H. Compton

Dr. Vannevar Bush was in charge of coordinating the government's scientific research. The reports of American physicist Dr. Arthur Compton had been instrumental in launching the Manhattan Project. The supposition in Dr. Compton's letter came as the result of a conference two days before between Compton and the scientists who made up the Theoretical Group in Chicago. At this meeting, the estimated time schedule for Germany's development of a nuclear weapon was agreed on. This time frame was largely based on bits and pieces of information that they were receiving from their contacts in Europe. The report from their meeting stated the following:

According to information received, the Germans began to receive 4 kg per day of heavy water from Norway on September 1, 1941. The amount of heavy water required for setting up a chain reaction depends on the amount and quality of uranium metal and other materials available, such as carbon. The estimates for the heavy water needed range from 620 to 1,000 kg, with a most probable amount of 800 kg...Assuming they will want to have about 15 bombs, from the first enriched plant, we can estimate that they would operate it until a total amount of 150 kg of 49 is reached in the plant.

Office of Scientific Research and Development
1530 P Street NW
Washington, D.C.

August 31, 1942

Major General George V. Strong
Assistant Chief of Staff, G2
War Department
Washington, D.C.

My Dear General Strong:

I mentioned certain long range developments in which the Germans are interested. I now have further information. A plant at Vemork [Norway] is producing 120 kilograms per month of one of the essential materials and shipping it to Berlin, and it then goes into the hands of Dr. Heisenberg, the distinguished physicist. This information comes from the British in rather devious ways. I hope the same information is getting to you directly and more completely...I also understand that the British are studying paying some attention to the Vemork plant.

I have a study going on from which I hope to give you further information soon about possible locations and the like for plants engaged on this matter...

Cordially yours,
V. Bush
Director

September 8, 1942

MEMORANDUM FOR GENERAL EISENHOWER

I am enclosing herewith a map of Norway showing the location of the town of Vemork, some four or five miles west of Rjukan. This town is the power center of Norway and contains three electric generating plants. Four photographs showing these installations are enclosed.

By the utilization of a portion of this power the Germans are now obtaining 120 kilograms of heavy water per month. This is being shipped to Berlin to be used for experimental purposes in the development of fission bombs based upon uranium.

Our own scientists are making progress along this line. My information indicated that British scientists are also making progress. It seems obvious from present developments that whichever nation can put fission bombs of this character in use will have a destructive agent which may determine the final outcome of this war.

It seems obvious that since there can be no production or development along this line without heavy water, that the designation of Vemork as a bombing objective from the air, or crippling of the plant by sabotage, should seriously be considered.

I have talked this over with Arnold and Handy and both agree with me that the matter should be called to your attention.

Geo. V. Strong
Major General
Assistant Chief of Staff, G-2

From these letters, as well as those written by Leo Szilard and signed by Albert Einstein, it becomes fairly obvious that the members of the atom-splitting scientists were somehow receiving information from Germany. It is likely that this information was coming from the English and American intelligence-gathering personnel in Europe and from the longtime personal friends of the scientists who were still in Germany.

THE IMPORTANCE OF HEAVY WATER

East Tennessee's Sven Nordquist (name changed at his request) spent twenty years in the U.S. Air Force and twenty years at Oak Ridge's Y-12 Nuclear plant. But Sven did not spend his early years in the United States. During the Depression, Sven moved with his Norwegian parents back to their native Oslo, Norway, in the hopes that they would find better economic conditions there.

Early in the morning of April 9, 1940, the Nordquist family watched from a porch balcony as German bombers filled the Norwegian sky. Sven remembers very well the sadness he felt when he saw tears streaming down his father's face. Initially, the Norwegians tried to fight back. A German battleship was sunk in one of the fjords between the Atlantic Ocean and Oslo. Sven's father listened to a small radio each night from a radio station broadcasting from England and passed the information to the underground fighters. His father and other men from their community went north to join guerrilla fighters. In several weeks, however, the entire country settled into the Nazi occupation for the duration. Sven's father, who survived several weeks fighting with the freedom fighters, met regularly with other men while they continued to plot possible ways of sabotaging their German occupiers.

Most Norwegians never knew that one of the biggest reasons the Germans came was to get water—heavy water. This unique water differs from normal water in that each of its hydrogen atoms has a neutron and a proton in its nucleus. In the hydrogen atom of regular water, there is only a proton in its nucleus. Therefore, heavy water really is heavier.

For several years, Norway's Norsk Hydro plant had been using the power of its abundant water as it fell from the steep mountains to make fertilizer. As a byproduct, heavy water was produced. Its customers were primarily the experimental laboratories throughout Europe. The unique water that it was producing was prized by scientists who were interested in nuclear fission. By 1938, scientists worldwide had become aware that if chain reactions could be controlled, atomic fission could become an important source of power. All that was needed was a substance that would "moderate" the energy of neutrons that were being emitted in radioactive decay. These neutrons could then be captured by other fissionable nuclei. Suddenly, heavy water became a likely candidate and in great demand. Interestingly, the Germans had given up on graphite, another good moderator, due to a mathematical error.

By the late 1930s, Adolf Hitler had become convinced that the country that was able to develop the atomic bomb first would almost certainly win the war. His interest in being the first to obtain the bomb is demonstrated over and over with his actions during a five-year period in Norway. With the occupation of Norway, the Germans controlled the largest heavy water plant in the world. This was of keen interest to two of their competitors, the United States and England.

The story of the Allies attempting to destroy the site and the Germans stubbornly bringing it back from the ashes was interesting enough to encourage Hollywood's production of *Heroes of Telemark*, a movie starring Kirk Douglas and Richard Harris. The series of assaults over a period of two years took ninety-two lives. Those attacks in chronological order follow:

- In Operation Grouse, a reconnaissance mission, an advance party of four Norwegian commandos parachuted to the top of a nearby plateau on October 18, 1942.
- Operation Freshman in November 1942 ended with disastrous results for the British. Thirty-four Royal Engineers from the 1st British Airborne Division and the crews of one bomber and two gliders died when they crashed into the side of a mountain because of poor visibility. A few survived but were tortured and executed by the Germans.
- On February 28, 1943, Norwegian commandos in a raid called Operation Gunnerside destroyed the plant along with five hundred kilograms of heavy water. Showing the importance of heavy water in Hitler's mind and his resolve to build an atomic bomb, the Germans stubbornly rebuilt the heavy water plant, which was in plain sight of American and English bombers.
- The Americans attempted to totally destroy the plant on November 16, 1943. An unprecedented 143 B-17 and B-24 bombers attacked the plant. The plant was not completely destroyed, but this raid was enough to cause the Germans to move the heavy water–making equipment to Germany early in 1944.
- A final operation was conducted by saboteurs of the Norwegian resistance forces on February 20, 1944. The heavy water that remained in Norway was being sent to Germany but went to the bottom of a fjord when the sabotaged ferry *D/F Hydro* exploded and sank. During the last days of the war in southern Germany, American soldiers came across pieces of the equipment from the Norway plant that had been salvaged from the many raids. The war ended before the equipment could be reassembled yet again.

CHAPTER 15

THE TWO MISSIONS THAT ENDED THE WAR

Hundreds of engineers worked furiously as they tried to get the mammoth B-29 bomber and the powerful P-51 fighter plane in the air as soon as it was practical. For the time, these airplanes epitomized the latest in aeronautical designs. No country in the world had a bomber so big and powerful and a fighter plane so fast that it could escort the bombers on most of their missions.

In other words, the designers of the nuclear weapons could not have asked for anything more. The B-29 gave them the needed large platform and the ability to fly great distances, and the P-51 fighter provided the perfect security escort.

The B-29 arrived just in time because the bombs they would be asked to carry weighed about ten thousand pounds. In March and June 1944, the air force practiced using its new release system by dropping dummy atomic bombs at the Glenn L. Martin plant in Omaha, Nebraska. After this successful exercise, the air corps modified seventeen B-29s that could meet the demands associated with carrying atomic weapons.

This group of planes and crew made up the 509th Composite Group. General "Hap" Arnold, the commanding general of the army air corps, appointed Lieutenant Colonel Paul Tibbetts to command this group. Tibbetts was a veteran B-17 pilot and had done extensive training in B-29s. Stationed at Wendover Field in Utah, the unit immediately started on a training program that would prepare it for its missions to the Japanese homeland.

The unit practiced for high-altitude drops of the bombs and an escape procedure that would lessen the expected shock waves that the planes were likely to encounter. In May 1945, the 509th deployed to the Pacific island of Tinian.

President Roosevelt, who had already appointed a target committee, died on April 12, 1945. The committee consisted of General Leslie Grove's deputy, two army air corps officers and five scientists and met three days after the death of Roosevelt. They made recommendations to the new president, Harry S Truman. Their initial list contained the names of seventeen Japanese cities, including Hiroshima and Nagasaki.

For some time, there had been a debate among scientists and political leaders, at least among those who knew the secret, about the ethics of using an atomic bomb without giving the enemy some type of warning. The case of those who had been strongly in favor of a warning, one that might include an actual demonstration of the power of the bomb, grew weaker when the horrible atrocities committed by Japanese soldiers on the islands of Iwo Jima, Tinian, Okinawa and other Pacific islands came to light. Further, America's military leaders estimated that an invasion of the Japanese island would cost a million American and Japanese lives.

In July 1945, the atomic bomb was tested at the Alamogordo Bombing Range south of Los Alamos, New Mexico. After this test, named "Trinity," was successful, the necessary parts for two different types of bombs, one with enriched uranium and one with plutonium, were carried to Tinian Island by the USS *Indianapolis* and by army air corps aircraft. Tinian Island was the closest island available for reaching the Japanese mainland.

Everything was ready by the first of August. President Truman, Secretary of War Henry Stimson and Army Chief of Staff George Marshall approved a directive that called for the missions to be carried out against the Japanese. Those who approved of the decision to go forward with the missions felt that the use of such a powerful new weapon would have a profound psychological effect on the enemy and hoped that this would bring about the end of the war without an all-out invasion being necessary. For them, this was of paramount importance.

By the evening of August 5, 1945, the uranium version of the atomic bomb, "Little Boy," was fully assembled and ready for arming once the B-29 was at altitude. Around midnight, the bomb was hoisted into the bomb bay of the bomber *Enola Gay*. The B-29, which carried the name of the mother of pilot Colonel Paul Tibbets, had a payload onboard that would likely alter the course of the war and, in so doing, change the world. The president along with Congressional and military leaders knew of the planned action and waited nervously for news.

At 2:45 a.m., the big bomber's four two-thousand-horsepower Wright Cyclone engines roared to life. Colonel Tibbets's radio indicated that all was well, and he was ready to go: "Dimples Eight Two to North Tinian Tower. Ready for takeoff on Runway Able." As they raced down the 8,500-foot runway, Tibbets held the plane's yoke down until they had reached 155 miles per hour before easing back and allowing the plane to start its climb that would eventually reach an altitude of 30,700 feet.

Strong shockwaves that could destroy the airplanes were a concern that went all the way back to the early planning stages of the missions. Scientists and air corps personnel estimated that the plane could survive the blast from a distance of eight miles. At about thirty-one thousand feet altitude, the plane would already be six miles in the air. To add to this distance, Tibbets decided that a quick 155-degree turn after the drop would be the best method.

Everyone concerned wanted the drop to accurately hit the target. Using the Norden bombsight, the bombardier was expected to put the bomb within two hundred feet of the actual target.

In addition to the *Enola Gay*, six other B-29s were a part of the mission. There was a standby plane, a photo plane, a plane carrying instruments to record the effects of the blast and three planes that scouted well ahead of Tibbets's plane. These three were on the lookout for enemy fighters while monitoring weather conditions. American P-51 Mustang fighters from Iwo Jima flew escort for the bombers. The *Great Artiste*, flown by Colonel Chuck Sweeney, carried the scientific instruments.

The scout planes reported light fighter resistance and that Hiroshima had only 30 percent cloud cover. With this information and with Hiroshima already being high on the list of potential targets, Tibbets quickly decided that it would be their target.

The *Enola Gay* lunged upward when the ten-thousand-pound payload fell from the airplane's bomb rack. By the time Tibbets had executed his 155-degree rapid turn and the bomb exploded, his B-29 was far enough away so that the only crewman to see the actual fireball was tail gunner Bob Caron. Even though he was wearing goggles, he immediately thought he had been blinded. When the shockwave, which was traveling at 1,100 feet per second, hit the veteran flyers, they said it felt like a near-miss from flak.

A mushroom cloud soared to forty-five thousand feet. A city lay in ruins; 140,000 Japanese died. Colonel Tibbets radioed to his superiors on Tinian Island that the primary target had been hit "with good results." Three days

Left: B-29 instrument panel (altimeters used Knoxville Native Weston Fulton's bellows). *Courtesy Air Force Museum.*

Below: Crew of *Bockscar*. *Back row, left to right*: Captain Kermit R. Beahan, bombardier; Captain James F. Van Pelt, navigator; Captain Charles D. Albury, pilot; Second Lieutenant Fred J. Olivi, co-pilot; and Major Charles W. Sweeney, aircraft commander. *Front row, left to right*: Staff Sergeant Edward K. Buckley, radar operator; Master Sergeant John D. Kuharek, flight engineer; Sergeant Raymond G. Gallagher, assistant flight engineer; Staff Sergeant Albert T. Dehart, tail gunner; Sergeant Abe M. Spitzer, radio operator. *Courtesy Air Force Museum.*

later, on August 9, 1945, Sweeney piloted *Bockscar* and dropped a plutonium-type bomb nicknamed "Fat Man" on Nagasaki.

Six days later, on August 15, 1945, the emperor of Japan agreed to the surrender terms that the Allies had laid out three weeks earlier. In his radio address, he told his countrymen that the Americans had used "a new and most cruel bomb, the power of which to do damage is incalculable." Because of this development and the current "war situation" for his country, he had decided that surrender was in Japan's best interest.

As the giant B-29s flew to and from their destinations, the fingerprints of East Tennesseans were abundant. The wings, fuselages and vertical and horizontal stabilizers were clad in aluminum made by the Aluminum Company of America, whose largest plant was located in Alcoa, Tennessee. The pilots and gunners peered through Plexiglas that was manufactured by Rohm and Haas Chemical Company, which had a major facility located just west of downtown Knoxville. A quarter of a mile from this plant was the sprawling Fulton Sylphon Company plant. From it came the more than one hundred bellows assemblies that the bombers had in their air frames and one bellows in each of their two altimeters. There were six bellows assemblies in their Norden bombsights, which made the sights so accurate. In the bomb bay, one of Fulton's bellows rode on each bomb as the main component in a barometric pressure switch, which was part of the system that caused the bombs to detonate at the optimum altitude of 1,890 feet. The uranium-235 that powered the first atomic bomb was enriched in Oak Ridge, Tennessee.

CHAPTER 16

TENNESSEANS AFTER THE WAR

Soon after the haughty celebrations at the end of the war, a sobering reality set in as thousands of defense-related jobs were no longer needed. While TVA was helping the economy of East Tennessee by providing relatively inexpensive electricity, the benefits were not enough to cause the creation of jobs for everyone. Because of this, many young people resumed their treks north to find work in the automobile manufacturing factories in Michigan and Ohio. They were doing exactly what so many of their parents had done prior to the war.

Some of the returning service men and women used their "mustering out" money to open small businesses. Typical of those businesses were delicatessens with their usual fare of foot-long hot dogs and French fries.

Because the GI Bill mandated that companies keep open the jobs for their returning veterans, thousands of women who had been in so much demand a few weeks earlier were told that they were no longer needed. They had proved, however, that they could work in a factory setting, and in many ways, this changed the American perception of working mothers. In spite of the disruptions, women's employment in the state showed an increase of twenty-three thousand by 1950.

Others used their money to purchase more modern equipment for their farms. Some even bought small farms. New tractors started replacing mules as the farmers' beast of burden. All the while, TVA was researching and developing better fertilizer that would help to make the crops of the farmers yield better.

After a few months of an adjustment period, the economy started improving dramatically. Suddenly, new houses were needed for the expanding families, and a new or used car became a necessity. Bank deposits tripled between 1940 and 1950. Personal income increased from about $1 billion in 1940 to nearly $3.3 billion in 1950.

As early as 1944, the State of Tennessee, once again leading the nation, began formulating a plan for re-assimilating its returning veterans. Later that same year, the U.S. Congress passed the Servicemen's Readjustment Act, which became better known as the GI Bill of Rights. It covered a veteran's tuition and expenses, thereby making college attainable for thousands of Tennesseans. Many became the first in their family to graduate from college. In this time of rapid change, they somehow found time to start the "baby boom" generation.

During the war, a rush to urbanization had taken place as people went to the cities for jobs. This move to the city became even more pronounced in the first years after the war. Tennessee's rural population decreased from about 1,272,000 in 1940 to approximately 1,000,000 by 1950. This trend continued, and by 1960, the farm population was less than 600,000.

Because so much of Tennessee was rural, with much of its population uneducated and untrained, even with an improved economy it would take several years for certain segments of the state's society to catch up with many other states. Everyone in the state had been affected in some way by the long war. Some had suffered terribly, but most Tennesseans would soon be affected in a positive way by the robust economic expansion.

Positioned as the gateway to the Great Smoky Mountains, the Gatlinburg/Pigeon Forge area of East Tennessee has become the nation's tenth top tourist destination. Several outstanding schools of higher learning and important industries have also allowed the area to participate fully in man's continuing quest for more and more technology.

EPILOGUE

The model who posed for Norman Rockwell's famous painting of *Rosie the Riveter* lived in Arlington, Vermont, where she met Rockwell, who lived in the nearby town of West Arlington. Mary Doyle Keefe was proud of her connection with the famous Rosie but preferred to keep a relatively low profile her entire life. She was paid five dollars each for her two sittings. Rockwell's Rosie died in Simsbury, Connecticut, from pneumonia on April 21, 2015.

The prolific inventor Weston Fulton sent so many patent applications in rapid succession to the United States Patent Office that the office set aside a room to exclusively handle his requests. The company that Fulton founded in 1904 operated for about one hundred years. A few years after being purchased by a leverage buyout company in 1986, it went into Chapter 11 bankruptcy. Once again on its feet, the company in the last few years has acquired two of its biggest competitors, and its business in general is expanding. It manufacturers several thousand bellows every day. From the long-ago days when it was used on Carl Norden's famous bombsight to its present-day NASA rocket applications, the legacy of the "Sylph" continues.

After the war, Rohm and Haas's contract with the government was canceled, and for four months, the government-owned plant was idle. In 1946, the company purchased the facility from the government. The Knoxville plant is still in operation but has not made Plexiglas since 1987. It has been acquired by Dow Chemical Company and currently is a major producer of several types of chemicals.

In spite of fierce competition, Alcoa continues to do well. Being prepared to meet the worldwide increase in the use of aluminum has helped considerably. From its earlier military clients, it has added an impressive list of civilian customers. Its products have applications that vary from sophisticated automobile parts to soft drink cans. By far the largest employer in Blount County, it continues to be a major economic driver in a large portion of East Tennessee.

The 1960s and 1970s were decades of unprecedented economic growth in the Tennessee Valley. By then, the natural resources that included land, water and timber had been largely restored, and Tennesseans were enjoying the benefits the resources were providing.

The Tennessee Valley Authority is still very important to most of Tennessee and parts of Georgia, Alabama and Kentucky. For years it has generated power using hydroelectric dams, coal-powered generators and nuclear power. Because of pressure from environmentalists, and in the interest of creating a cleaner environment, it is phasing out many of its coal-powered units. It has fewer than half of the employees it had at one time.

Albert Einstein, the famous physicist who through the subterfuge letters that he signed helped convince President Roosevelt of the need to quickly pursue nuclear weapons before the Germans had an opportunity to develop them, died on April 18, 1955.

After the war ended, Paul Tibbets remained in the air force. In 1947, the United Stated Air Force became a separate organization and was no longer part of the army. Tibbets soon qualified to fly America's first all-jet bomber, the B-47, which he flew for three years. He served at several air bases around the world and eventually reached the rank of brigadier general. He was asked to be an advisor for the Hollywood movie *Above and Beyond* and was glad that Robert Taylor played him. Tibbets was a popular speaker for the rest of his life. He died in Columbus, Ohio, on November 1, 2007.

Chuck Sweeney also continued flying after the war and also became a general. He flew F-86 Saber jets for the Massachusetts Air National Guard for several years. During the 1961 Berlin Crisis, he was the wing commander of three squadrons of fighter planes at the Phalsbourg, Air Force Base in eastern France. One of the writers of this work, Dewaine Speaks, served under Sweeney's command at that time. During a conversation with Speaks, the general mentioned that he had been only twenty-three years old when he flew the second atomic bomb mission. Before retiring in 1976 from the National Guard, Sweeney reached the rank of major general. He died in Boston at the age of eighty-four on July 16, 2004.

Navigator Theodore "Dutch" Van Kirk, who was the last surviving crew member of the *Enola Gay*, died in 2014 at the age of ninety-two.

The National Guard's 30th Division, of which the 117th Infantry Regiment was a part, served with distinction in several battles in Europe. After the war, the 30th Division was named the number-one infantry division in the European Theater.

The Shinkolobwe mine was officially closed by Congo's president on January 28, 2004. Nonetheless, local people still attempt to do illegal mining there. Later in 2004, eight died when the roof of the old mine collapsed. In 2006, the *Sunday Times* reported that Iran was seeking to import "bomb-making uranium" from the Shinkolobwe mine.

Tennessee senator Kenneth D. McKellar was chairman of the Senate Appropriations Committee and secretly found funding for the Manhattan Project in concert with President Roosevelt. He became the unofficial vice president of the United States while also serving as president of the Senate. The mechanism was not yet in place whereby President Truman could appoint a vice president on his own. Due to this situation, the Twenty-fifth Amendment to the Constitution of the United States remedied this anomaly. Senator McKellar served in the Senate until 1953 and died in 1957 at age eighty-eight.

Cordell Hull, the former secretary of state who had been given the opportunity to become Roosevelt's vice president instead of Harry S Truman, died in the Bethesda Naval Hospital on July 23, 1955.

In June 1945, the "Old Hickory Division" turned the sector it controlled over to the Russians. The Russians occupied this territory until 1989, when the Berlin Wall came down and the Cold War officially ended.

The German and Italian prisoners of war who were held at Camp Crossville were returned to their home country in 1946. Eleven of the escapees had been caught by 1951. The last holdout did not surrender until 1985.

Tennessee Eastman Company is now a separate company called Eastman Chemical Company. It remains a large producer of chemicals and remains a major employer in the upper East Tennessee area.

Holston Ordnance is now called Holston Army Ammunition Plant. For a while during the Vietnam War, it was hard-pressed to meet the demands of the military. It is still in operation.

Kingsport, Tennessee, is a modern city that still benefits from the way it was planned and the way its leaders were able to recruit industries with good-paying jobs. As would be expected with all of the professional people in the city, Kingsport's schools are excellent.

After the war, Oak Ridge's X-10 plant became Oak Ridge National Laboratory. It is the nation's leading laboratory in research regarding nuclear power and nuclear medicine. It continues to do research in physics and produce radioactive isotopes for science and industry.

During the Cold War, Oak Ridge played an important role in keeping America's nuclear weapons ready in case they were needed. Since then, research in the areas of nuclear medicine, nuclear power and radioisotopes have been more of their focus.

Dr. Vannevar Bush was the government's coordinator of scientific research during the war. After the war, he helped promote the importance of science in the postwar era. He died in Belmont, Massachusetts, on June 28, 1974.

Dr. Arthur H. Compton was a key physicist in the development of nuclear weapons. Following the war, he became chancellor of Washington University in St. Louis. He died in Berkeley, California, at sixty-nine on March 15, 1962.

The Clinchfield Railroad that was so important when George Eastman was choosing East Tennessee for his major chemical plant is still operating but is now a division of CSX Railroad Company.

In 1949, "Sven Nordquist" returned to America, but his parents remained in Norway.

By 1944, the United States had accumulated twenty tons of heavy water even though at the time it relied more heavily on graphite as a neutron moderator. Over the years, heavy water has remained a prized commodity worldwide.

Knoxville's Worth Campbell, who learned of the end of the war while on a Liberty ship, met and thanked Paul Tibbets for dropping the first atomic bomb that helped save Campbell from having to participate in the planned all-out invasion of Japan.

The Volunteer Army Ammunition Plant was kept in standby condition for six years. In 1952, the plant was reactivated and remained in operation until 1957, when its production ceased and the plant was placed in "protective surveillance." During the Vietnam War, the plant was opened yet again and remained operational until the end of that war. The site is now the home of a Volkswagen manufacturing facility.

Jack Westbrook stayed in the Air Force Reserve and retired with the rank of colonel. He went back to school under the GI Bill and graduated from the University of Tennessee in 1949 with a major in journalism. He married Winnie in 1950. During his long career, Jack was awarded the following medals: Meritorious Service Medal, Air Medal with two Oak Leaf Clusters,

Army Commendation Medal, Distinguished Unit Citation, Organizational Excellence Award, Army Good Conduct Medal, American Campaign Ribbon, Asiatic-Pacific Campaign Ribbon, WWII Victory Medal, Army of Occupation Medal, Air Force Longevity Ribbon, Armed Forces Reserve Medal, Small Arms Expert Marksmanship Award and National Defense Service Medal. Jack and Winnie live in west Knoxville.

The former medic Homer Stooksbury worked several years at the Oak Ridge complex and retired from TVA after twenty more years. He lives in the Knoxville area.

In 2009, the City of Oak Ridge Public Library received fourteen rolls of microfilm tapes from the National Archives in Washington, D.C. The declassified "SECRET" letters used in this work came from those tapes.

BIBLIOGRAPHY

Ames Historical Society. "World War II Rationing on the U.S. Homefront." May 9, 2015. http://www.ameshistory.org/exhibits/events/rationing.htm.

Blee, C.E. "Development of the Tennessee River Waterway." Paper presented to Society of Civil Engineers. Chicago, September 12, 1952.

Collins, Dave. "Rosie the Riveter Model Dies at 92." *Knoxville News Sentinel*, April 26, 2015.

Cryptome. "Nuclear Weapons Arming and Fuzing." February 22, 2015. http://cryptome.org/nuke-fuze.htm.

Dobbs, Michael. *Saboteurs*. New York: Random House, 2004.

Global Security. "Vemork Heavy Water Plant—1942–44." July 1, 2015. http://www.globalsecurity.org/wmd/ops/vemork.htm.

Herr, Kincaid. *The Louisville & Nashville Railroad*. Louisville, KY: L&N Public Relations Department, First Printing April, 1943.

Kieman, Denise. *The Girls of Atomic City*. New York: Simon & Schuster, 2013.

The Manhattan Project. October 8, 2015. http://.osti.gov/manhattan-project-history/Events/1942-1944_ur/navy_ltd.htm.

National Archives. World War II Microfilm Tapes. The City of Oak Ridge Public Library, 2009. General collection from the National Archives and can be viewed in the reference section of the City of Oak Ridge library.

National Museum of the U.S. Air Force. "Fat Man" Atomic Bomb, May 16, 2015. http://www.nationalmuseum.af.mil.

The National World War II Museum. "V-Mail." August 2015. New Orleans, LA. http://www.nationalww2museum.org.

Nichols, Ruth D. "Civilian Conservation Corps (CCC)." Tennessee Encyclopedia of History and Culture, May 28, 2015. http://tennesseeencyclopedia.net/entry.php?rec=266.

Present, Thelma. *Letters to Margaret.* Knoxville: East Tennessee Historical Society, 1985.

Shaw, James P., IV. "Historic Preservation in a New Town: Oak Ridge, Tennessee." Master's thesis, University of Tennessee, March 1988.

Stephens, Dr. Ruth. "The Aluminum Company of America." WKGN recorded radio broadcast. Knoxville, TN, December 22 and 29, 1957.

Tennessee Valley Authority. *Part I: TVA Innovations & Inventions 1933 to 1948.* Knoxville, TN: self-published, n.d.

———. "TVA—The 1940s." https://www.tva.com/About-TVA/Our-History/The-1940s.

30th Infantry Division, 177th Infantry Regiment, HRS, World War II Reenactors. "117th Infantry Regiment—HRS." December 14, 2015. http://30thhrs.org/contact.html.

30th Infantry Division Veterans of World War II. June 19, 2015. http://30thinfantry.org/index2.shtml.

United States History. "Cordell Hull." May 28, 2015. http://www.u-s-history.com/pages/h1630.html.

———. "U.S. War Bonds." June 19, 2015. http://www.u-s-history.com/pages/h1682.html.

U.S. Atomic Energy Commission. *The First Reactor.* Pamphlet. Oak Ridge, TN, n.d.

Volunteer Army Ammunition Plant. *Historic American Engineering Record.* Washington, D.C.: Department of the Interior, n.d.

Wessels Living History Farm. "Farming in the 1940s." http://www.livinghistoryfarm.org/farminginthe40s/farminginthe1940s.html.

———. "Rationing & Scrap Drives." June 22, 2015. http://www.livinghistoryfarm.org/farminginthe40s/lifeo9.html.